Follow GOD'S Plan and Stop Making SENSE

Be Yourself

LAWRENCE KINNY

PARTRIDGE
A Penguin Random House Company

To order additional copies of this book, contact
Toll Free 800 101 2657 (Singapore)
Toll Free 1 800 81 7340 (Malaysia)
orders.singapore@partridgepublishing.com

www.partridgepublishing.com/singapore

This book will help you find out who you are,
bring in alignment your goals, values, work and purpose in life.

CONTENTS

Part One: Self Educate

Part Two: Step up

Part Three: Manage Your Mind and Emotions

ACKNOWLEDGEMENTS

I would like to thank my Parents Richard Kinny & Ruby Nazareth for giving me the freedom and support to make my own choices in life. My Grandmother Flory Kinny for making sure I read the Bible and engrained in me the need to pray and fear God in my early days, May her soul rest in peace. I would like to thank my Sister & brother Anita Kinny and Simon Kinny for their love and support. I would like to thank all the friends who have been and are a part me.

I would like to thank my wife Yolanda for all her support and love during testing times and still believing in me. I would like to thank my children Daniel and Sarah for giving me a reason to be inspired. I would above all like to thank God for all the opportunities he has given me and for shaping, moulding and sculpting me.

"It's no wonder that truth is stranger than fiction.
Fiction has to make sense."
—Mark Twain

We must need what we want.
The life that is, needs to be enjoyed;
The life that we want needs to be worked upon.
When we need to know who we are, we need to create goals!
To find the answers within, we need intuition and trained
    instincts.
To begin, we need courage; to strive forward, we need faith.
To know what's possible, we need to believe in ourselves.
To feel, we need a heart; to see, we need to have a vision.
To achieve daily goals, we need to focus.
Joys and successes are needed to empower us;
Failure is feedback telling us that we need to change.
The journey is our reward, when we need to find our purpose in
    life.
Becoming who we need to be is God's will!

PART ONE

SELF EDUCATE

KNOW YOURSELF

"You create your own universe as you go along."
—Winston Churchill

Know Yourself

"You have to look at yourself objectively. Analyze yourself like an instrument. You have to be absolutely frank with yourself. Face your handicaps, don't try to hide them. Instead, develop something else."—Audrey Hepburn

Knowing yourself is the beginning of your journey. Everything people do, think, or act upon will be from the point of view of who they think they are. The knowledge about who you really are will provide greater clarity about your strengths and weaknesses, and the direction you need to take in life. People need to be careful about who they think they are; this will also determine how far a person will go in life. Another simpler perspective to this is your self-image: how do you see yourself? It's not how others see you—it's how you perceive yourself in your mind and what do you think you deserve in life. The important part to know about self-image is that you can consciously change it anytime; it may not be effective immediately, with repetition it will become you, and you will become it. Take a moment to introspect and find out who you think you really are, and write down the answers. Do not proceed to the next step until you get some clarity on who you think you are.

> "Knowing others is intelligence; knowing yourself is true wisdom. Mastering others is strength; mastering yourself is true power. If you realize you have enough you are truly rich."—Lao Tzu

Let us understand first why it is important to know yourself. If you know yourself, it will be easier to find out what makes you happy and sad and why; it will then be much easier for you to know how you operate and what changes you will need to make. First we must understand and accept that we are all humans. Why is this important? Because it allows us to get up when we fail; we are bound to make mistakes, and we *should* make mistakes because no one is perfect. We should not allow ourselves to be beaten down by guilt or failure; we must learn and move on. Being human allows us to accept that we do not have all the answers; it allows us to leave the things that we don't understand upon God and to work towards things that we understand. The journey is to find out who we really are, why we are, and what we want to be. It is a process, and we will keep learning and realizing our potential as we introspect daily.

We will grow in our strengths and be able to strengthen our weaknesses. You can begin with the knowledge and experience that you already have available for reference. Your learning and experiences from the past will guide you and are priceless resources for self-knowledge.

Begin writing down answers to questions such as: Why did God choose you to be where you are today? What has God being preparing you for so far? How have your experiences in the past made you stronger and wiser? What are your strengths and weaknesses? Even though you may not have clear answers immediately, keep asking these questions to yourself until you start getting some clarity. Dig into yourself week after week. The purpose of this is to know yourself and to give you fair clarity about who you are, as opposed to who you *think* you are. There is a big difference between the two. Sometimes you may think you are a certain kind of a person, whereas your values might be completely different from what you think you are. Your job is to get answers and synchronize the two answers about who you think you are and who you really are. The answers to these questions for me would be something like, "I am kind person, I am enterprising, and I love helping people." The response tells me that this is fairly true about who I really am. I will need to synchronize these values with who I think I am.

"He who knows others is wise; he who knows himself is enlightened."—Lao Tzu

Who are the people you admire, either from history or still living, and why? What are the qualities about them you admire the most? The answers to these questions will help you connect with your values and create a plan of how you can achieve your values. The answers will start the process of knowing yourself. My role model is Jesus Christ, and I like the work done by Mahatma Gandhi, Mother Teresa, and Martin Luther King Jr, so I know deep down inside that my values and happiness are connected with the kind of work they carried out. If I work on even partly similar lines, I will be happier, fulfilled, and truly rich. Your answers will differ; however, it will help you understand many things about yourself and your values, so write down any names that comes to your mind—be honest and expect a whole new world to open up for you. Don't worry about whether or not you understand it; keep doing it until you are certain. You will not understand it in one go, but with repetition it will all come together. It's a process, and you will need to make changes and adjustments with new insights, just like a plane changing course to reach a particular destination. Set the process in action by answering a few of the questions I have listed.

- Where do you live? Where do you want to live? What kind of house do you want to live in? Why?
- What car do you drive? Which car would you like to drive? Why?
- Where do you work? Where would you like to work? Why?
- What Kind of work do you do? What kind of work would you like to do? Why?

Your answers to the above questions will give you more clarity on who you are. Who you would like to be like? What drives you? What makes you happy? What's important for you? Answering the "why" can get you in touch with the feelings and emotions that you want to fulfil upon achieving your goals, and because they are attached to some of your values you're seeking to accomplish. They will also help you prioritize your goals and identify the immediate goals and changes needed.

Love and Respect Yourself

"I will not let anyone walk through my mind with dirty feet."—Mahatma Gandhi

As Buddha said, "No one saves us but ourselves. No one can and no one may. We ourselves must walk the path." You are unique, and there is no one on the entire planet like you; no one can do things exactly the way you do them. What makes you unique from the rest of the world is your perception, and the way you look at the world is based on your experiences (good or bad), your environment, your upbringing, and more. When your upbringing and environment of growth were still the same as your siblings and the other children who grew up with you, even so, in a situation each one of you saw it so differently and acted differently. This explains how unique and blessed you are by God in your own unique ways, and once you understand this, you can then take control and change your perceptions. Feel the blessings of the almighty in the form of your existence, learn to love and respect yourself. You must appreciate, love, and respect your own blessings first, before you can expect the world to do the same. The way you treat yourself and behave sets the benchmark for how others should treat you. If you wish to know how much your existence is affecting other people's lives, I recommend you watch the movie *It's a Wonderful Life*.

"Every saint has a past and every sinner has a future."—Oscar Wilde

I started by first making a statement: begin the journey of knowing yourself by accepting the fact that you are human. The reason for the statement is that people must first understand that they will never be perfect; they can only evolve and excel. People make wrong decisions, act badly, and make mistakes. It is not because they want to—nobody wants to look stupid or suffer humiliation and failure. People usually use their existing knowledge and experience to the best of their abilities, to deal with their challenges and situations. Sometimes this may backfire and cause embarrassment because of a lack of expertise. I have made many mistakes in my life, and do you think it was because I wanted to? No, and the same is true with anybody else. I had to take responsibilities very early in life with limited knowledge, help, and experience to draw upon. Do you think I wanted to take on these responsibilities? No, but I had to. The responsibilities I should have faced when I was thirty, I had to face at the age of sixteen. My whole life turned upside down, and I went through a depression and went bankrupt. I lost all my self-confidence and self-esteem, and I started hating myself, but I never gave up because I knew God would take care of things eventually.

It takes time for our wounds to heal, but guilt haunts us forever and takes us down a bad path as it becomes our dominant thought. You can change everything around by focusing on empowering thoughts. When I hit rock bottom, I knew that the only way was up. I started seeking help and knowledge through books, which gave me tools about how I could change my way of focus through meditation, daydreaming, and self-suggestion. I had to let go of all the guilt and bad memories because I could not live in self-imprisonment anymore. I started implementing the knowledge I learned with activities that would make me feel empowered, happy, and enthusiastic daily, until it became a habit. As the Dalai Lama said, "The purpose of our lives is to be happy." I had to gather my courage to get out of self-imprisonment and began doing things that made me happy. I started feeling good because I was building more good memories to reflect upon. Over a period of time, I got my self-confidence and self-esteem back because I simply felt good about myself.

It takes time, but as long as you have courage to change things, God will help you to get through no matter what. It is like planting new seeds and watering them everyday until you will start seeing results. As I started loving and respecting myself again, my world changed. You can start today by simply making a decision in your heart and working on yourself. Set yourself free by forgiving yourself and taking control of the direction of your life. Love and respect yourself and show it to the world, and the world will treat you how you want them to treat you. As Confucius said, "Respect yourself, and others will respect you." The world will first see how you treat yourself and decide to treat you accordingly. Occasionally do things that elevate you, gift yourself with doing things that make you happy, and let yourself know how much you appreciate and love yourself. When people ask you how you are doing, you can say something like "Great" or "Fabulous" because you will have something to live up to.

> "You cannot be lonely if you like the person you are alone with."—Wayne Dyer

Respect others:

> "I speak to everyone in the same way, whether he is the garbage man or the president of the university."—Albert Einstein.

True self-esteem comes from a place when a person does not think anybody is inferior or superior to him. People must also respect everyone they meet because a person's value lies in how much he loves and respects others, and not on how much money he has in the bank account. If we disrespect others, then we can expect the same back, as it is said in the Bible: "Treat others as you would like them to treat you." Luke 6:31 People have their own lives with their own shares of challenges and downfalls; with this perspective, it will be easier for us to give others a benefit of doubt and practice kindness and compassion towards everyone, as Plato said centuries ago: "Be kind; everyone you meet is fighting a hard battle." We are all passing through life with our own individual trials. All of us are connected to each other because we occupy physical, mental, and spiritual space in the world. What we say or do affects others around us and creates a ripple effect; and therefore it is our individual responsibility to create a positive ripple effect. Let me share a small piece I read which will explain why people must respect everyone, and what kind of an environment it can eventually create when the ripple effect starts.

The Messiah in Disguise

High in the mountains was a monastery that had once been known throughout the world. Its monks were pious, its students were enthusiastic. The chants from the monastery's chapel deeply touched the hearts of people who came there to pray and meditate.

But something had changed. Fewer and fewer young men came to study there; fewer and fewer people came for spiritual nourishment. The monks who remained became disheartened and sad.

Deeply worried, the abbot of the monastery went off in search of an answer. Why had his monastery fallen on such hard times?

The abbot came to a guru, and he asked the master, "Is it because of some sin of ours that the monastery is no longer full of vitality?"

"Yes," replied the master, "it is the sin of ignorance."

"The sin of ignorance?" questioned the abbot. "Of what are you ignorant?"

The guru looked at the abbot for a long, long time, and then he said, "One of you is the messiah in disguise. But, you are all ignorant of this." Then, the guru closed his eyes, and he was silent.

"The messiah?" thought the abbot. "The messiah is one of us? Who could it be? Could it be Brother Cook? Could it be Brother Treasurer? Could it be Brother Bell-Ringer? Could it be Brother Vegetable Grower? Which one? Which one? Every one of us has faults, failings, human defects. Isn't the messiah supposed to be perfect? But, then, perhaps these faults and failings are part of his disguise. Which one? Which one?"

When the abbot returned to the monastery, he gathered all the monks together and told them what the guru had said.

"One of us? The messiah? Impossible!"

But the master had spoken, and the master was never wrong.

"One of us? The messiah? Incredible! But, it must be so. Which one? Which one? That brother over there? That one? That one?"

Whichever one of the monks was the messiah, he was surely in disguise.

Not knowing who amongst them the messiah, all the monks began treating each other with new respect. "You never know," they thought. "He might be the one, so I had better deal with him kindly."

It was not long before the monastery was filled with newfound joy. Soon, new students came to learn, and people came from far and wide to be inspired by the chants of the kind, smiling monks.

Once again, the monastery was filled with the spirit of love.

From the story it becomes pretty clear of how a small change in perception towards another person can start a ripple effect which can affect a family, neighbourhood, a community, a city and a country in a positive direction. The potential of a positive change begins when we start respecting each other doesn't matter who it is as J. K. Rowling said, "If you want to know what a man's like, take a good look at how he treats his inferiors, not his equals." Start working on respecting and loving others first in the family because if people don't respect and love their family members then can they truly respect anyone outside of the family. People must first begin this ripple in the family.

Find your Values;

> "Your beliefs become your thoughts,
> your thoughts become your words,
> your words become your actions,
> your actions become your habits,
> your habits become your values
> and your values become your destiny."
> —Mahatma Gandhi

Values are something that people hold dear to them on a deeper level. Values are like the guiding system with which people assess a situation, create personal desires, and get angry when one of them is violated. Whatever people desire and want is driven by their values, because every goal is underpinned by values. If you want to know what your values are, look at the list of your goals you have created and ask yourself, what will you get by achieving your goals? Will you feel secure, happy, loved, or responsible? The answer will direct you to the value you are pursuing through the goal. Your goals must include you in them for the goals to be personal, because if your goals are not personal and you do not figure in the accomplishments of your goals, you may lose your desire to achieve them. What I mean is that people have goals and desires to provide for their loved ones, and they work until their graves to accomplish it without having themselves in the picture, which causes a disconnect with their own values.

I'd love to own a four-bedroom apartment facing the sea with a swimming pool, and I'd love to drive a Range Rover. This desire lets me know that I value abundance, happiness, and security. I am passionate about motivational speaking, being kind, and helping people—those are my core values which drive me, and this tells me about my passion and the career I must pursue in line with my values. If I get angry at someone for not being loyal to me, that means I value loyalty. We all have a certain set of values we treasure, and our values are personal because every person is unique. Your values will depend about what you expect from your life. Your values could be as simple as being a responsible citizen, neighbour, father, mother, son, or daughter, and so you put all your energy trying to live up to your values. You always get what you expect in life, because life is a self-fulfilling prophecy. You may want to be financially independent, and that means you value security. After getting clarity on your values, you will find it helps to choose the direction of your life, and you will also be willing to pay any price to live up to your own expectations.

Life only gives us what we expect and work to get. We either live up to our expectations or not; however, knowing what values we are pursuing will make it much easier to pursue our goals. Knowing our values will also eventually figure out our life's purpose. By the time you finish this book, it will become much clearer. If you are pursuing goals and somehow have not yet accomplished them, or you are not happy with the results, then it's time for you to check whether your values are supporting you in your pursuit. In pursuit of happiness, we must be in alignment with our thoughts, goals, passion, values, actions, and environment, like the tires of the car need to be aligned in order to move smoothly in one direction.

I was unhappy for the longest time in my job as a customer service representative for a bank, because it was not where my heart was; my values were not being fulfilled, and I was not moving in the direction of my goals. My environment did not help me grow personally, professionally, or spiritually. I had to make a choice to turn things around, and I started seeking a path that would support and bring me in alignment. I started a network marketing business, and when I found that my values were still contradicting with what I was doing, I decided to become an author. People are unique, and what worked for me may not work for others because their values may be different from mine.

Everything that is worth accomplishing in life is revolving around people's values. Evaluate and write down your goals and find out the values underpinned by these goals to get clarity and to understand the direction of your life. I do this exercise with people I work with every week until they start getting clarity on their values, goals, and passion. Find your values in life (professional, personal, and spiritual), align them and create your goals, and direct and design your life by being true to yourself.

Find Your Strengths and Talents

"Know thy self, know thy enemy. A thousand battles, a thousand victories."—Sun Tzu

Our strengths are our pillars in troubled times, and the fact is all of us have a list of strengths. List the strengths you are aware of, whatever comes to your mind at first, and do it week after week so that you can get clarity on your strengths and more knowledge of what you can fall back on during adversity. Life is full of ups and downs, and in the words of Albert Camus, "In the depth of winter, I finally learned that within me there lay an invincible summer." Listing your strengths will give you a fair idea on them. This process will also highlight the strengths, skills, and characteristics you would like to have and that you don't have yet; this will help you to further work on yourself to become the person you truly want to be. Once you have identified the strengths and skills you want to have, you can then find people who have those strengths and skills, and acquire them by reading about them, using these people as role models, spending more time with them, and seeking advice.

Make a list of all your talents that you can contribute to making the world around you a better place. Make a list of all the times you felt the adrenaline, felt great and at your peak performance, and find out why you felt so great during these moments. This list will give you clarity about what you would like to do and be as this is your passion. You will need to make this list and work on it week after week to get more clarity on your strengths and skills you have, as well as the one's you would like to acquire for your success in the goals you are pursuing.

Make a List of Your Role Models Whom You Would Like to Emulate

> "Tell me who your role models are and what you pay attention to, and I can tell you what you would like to do and be like."

Make a list of all your role models, alive or dead, and why you admire these people. Again, you need to make this list week after week until you are certain about the skills and characteristics you need to acquire from your role models. You can learn different skills from different people; choose wisely what skills or characteristics you would like to learn from each and list them down. You may have seen music lovers who have posters of music bands and idols in their bedrooms. You will need to create a similar environment to help you see your role models every day and to remind you of who you want to be like. For example, children are the best at role modelling without inhibitions. As Confucius said many centuries ago, "By three methods you may learn wisdom: First, by reflection, which is noblest; second, by imitation, which is easiest; and third, by experience, which is the bitterest." Choose the method your wish to use to acquire your wisdom.

Role modelling is the second method of imitation, which is the easiest. As children we are born with this natural capability of learning through role modelling. For example, we learned to walk, speak, and behave by watching our parents. As children grow, they role model their favourite superheroes and cartoon characters. After college, when people get stuck into a rut and reality kills their imagination, people forget about this great, god-given gift. We need to start using it again. For example, have you ever spent may be several hours watching movies or television programs, and after that you find yourself speaking, acting, and behaving like the characters you've been watching? This is a process of the unconscious learning abilities you have, which we will discuss later in the book.

Having the list of my role models helps me to determine the kind of work I would like to be involved in, and in which direction my learning should be focused. In order to copy them, I read their books, watch videos, and gather as much information available online, to know how they think and operate. Whatever vivid answers you may have, write them down and understand why you chose them. This will set the process of self-discovery in motion.

Make a List of Your Favourite Movies

> "The movies you love and admire are to some extent a function of who you are when you see them."—Mary Schmich

Movies you watch have a great impact on you and on your thinking patterns, because movies greatly influence society. Have you ever wondered why people like some movies, and why they don't like others, no matter what the expert opinions are about them? It's probably because the movie touched a part of their own story somewhere. Some movies move us emotionally and bring tears, others make us laugh, and some make no difference at all. Movies we love also tell a little bit about who we think we are. Make a list of your favourite movies, and write down what you liked about these movies and how it relates to your life and your values. You will be surprised at the answers you will get. Write them down week after week to know yourself. I like the movie *Seabiscuit* because of the struggle, achievement, spirit, and friendship, so I know now how I relate to movies and the values I perceive in them. Make a list and see what your answers are. As David Ansen noted, "We are the movies and the movies are us."

Find out What Drives You in Life

> "All children are artists. The problem is how to remain an artist once he grows up."—Pablo Picasso

Most children were very passionate about a lot of things; there was often joy and fun in doing things, until they grew up into adults and lost that joy, fun, and art along the way. We all are unique with unique talents, and we can discover them if we are willing to spend time with ourselves on a daily or weekly basis, to find out what really drives us and makes us happy in life. Our job is to find out what we enjoy doing so much that we lose track of time in accomplishing it; we will lose ourselves to find ourselves. It's like falling in love for the first time over and over again, which will stimulate us to break our boundaries, make us dance on thin ice effortlessly, and make our pain seem like pleasure. It's where the heart will sing and the mind will dance in synchronization, in a state of bliss and magic. Passion is needed for happiness, happiness is needed for success, and success is needed for the fulfilment of desires underpinned by our values.

The most important quest for me in my journey has been to find the things I would do for free, just to feel the adrenaline rush and to feel alive. I found that in writing, reading, and helping people; I find a certain sense of worth and fulfilment in these activities. It has been a long journey; however, all I can say is that it is totally worth the risk and the pain I took. The reason I am writing this book with my experiences is to empower people to find their passion much faster than I did. I already know the road map for me, and by sharing my experiences with others, I will be able to help them find their own road maps. Passion brings out our heart into play the human spirit, which operates out of joy in the face of challenges and the unknown. That passion gives us strength to endure and courage to pursue our goals with hope in the face of fear, and it leads us through the darkest places to the greatest achievements and fulfilment in life, knowing we are making a difference. You can find out what your passion is and what drives you in life by asking yourselves a few questions. What would you rather do if you had all the money in the world and did not have to work for money? What are the things that you would like to do in your spare time that will make you lose track of time? These are a couple of questions to begin with; you can come up with your own questions to dig into yourself. I am sure you've a got the gist of how to go about it, and the fact that you are reading this book says that you are willing and seeking. My experiences will only shed light on what already exists in you—finding it is your decision, so spend time and invest in yourself.

Believe in Yourself

"Believe in yourself and there will come a day when others will have no choice but to believe with you."—Oscar Wilde

Conviction in what you do and what you stand for will deliver you through all the challenges and take you through to the finish line. Conviction will increase your confidence, and confidence will help you break through. I had heard many motivational speakers make this statement: "Believe in yourself." I thought I understood it all and knew how to do it, but what I didn't realize was that believing in yourself is a process, too, and it happens in stages—you cannot fake it because it has to be felt. One morning after I woke up, I truly understood this statement. Believing in myself is all about being confident, and it has to be felt in order to reflect in my body language, working together as a unit.

People who believe in themselves are not afraid because they are focused on the task at hand. This is the secret ingredient in the success of achieving our goals. If you meet people who are successful, you will notice their conviction and confidence in themselves, and you will see this in how they walk, speak, and behave: everything is in synchronization, as if it is effortless. It seems effortless because they have found their treasure within: conviction and confidence. Confidence is needed when we are not 100 per cent sure of success. If we knew we were going to be successful, then we wouldn't need confidence and could just do it. Confidence and conviction is tested in the face of uncertainty.

I started with humble beginnings as a waiter to support my studies, after a heartbreak I decided to prove myself, so I decided to enter show business and become a Disc Jockey. I had absolutely no idea if I would be successful but I believed in the value I was pursuing through the goal and I believed in myself. In the seven years that I was a DJ, I worked as freelance DJ, learned about all the technical aspects of sound set up and playing for various private parties learned about different kinds of Music for three years. As a natural progression I decided to play professionally and joined a company as a professional DJ, I was sacked within a month saying that I cannot become a professional DJ. I just got even more mad and pursued being a DJ aggressively and in four years I was a Professional DJ, handling a popular club in Mumbai and popularly known as DJ Larry. Gave interviews on two national television networks, had many write ups in popular tabloids in Mumbai including Bombay times of Times of India and Mid-day in the year 2000. In the year 2000 I had achieved my goal after seven years and now I had proved myself.

I had to believe in myself and the goals I was pursuing, I just needed to achieve my values and I never gave myself any other choice. What everyone thought about me didn't matter to me, when everyone was laughing at me it didn't matter. All I knew was I had to prove myself because the pain of not proving myself was much more then the pain of proving myself, and I did. Ask yourself if the pain of not achieving your goals is much more then the pain of achieving your goals? What are you willing to do and how are you going to do it? When you believe in yourself, you will find the confidence which will then transform into conviction and then whatever you do your conviction will reflect in the way you speak, act and behave in synchronisation. Eventually you will accomplish your goals and values bringing you more happiness. As Swami Vivekananda had said "You cannot believe in God until you believe in yourself."

INTUITION

"I believe in intuitions and inspirations . . .
I sometimes *feel* that I am right. I do not *know* that I am."
—Albert Einstein

As Per "Wikipedia" Intuition is the ability to acquire knowledge without inference or the use of reason. The word "intuition" comes from the Latin word "intueri", which is often roughly translated as meaning "'to look inside" or "to contemplate".

Intuition, as generally understood, would be about having a strong feeling that certain things are about to happen; you know it but don't know how. It could be a bad or a good thing about to happen. You feel it within without knowing how and before those events occur; you can also call it the sixth sense. In this chapter I will be specifically speaking about intuition in the context of seeking answers. Intuition needs to be experienced in order to understand how it works.

Let me explain how intuition worked for me so that I may be able to make it simpler for you to understand. In my twelfth grade in the year 1995, my circumstances started deteriorating rapidly, and I just could not understand why this was happening to me. I needed answers to questions so that I could resolve to live happier, and after a lot of contemplation, there it was: I remembered that my grand mom had vowed to visit the holy shrine of Our Lady of Vailankanni (Mother Mary) in Chennai, in South India, if I passed the tenth grade, which I did a couple of years ago. I thought, "Maybe that's the reason things aren't going my way." I was desperate for things to get better, and so I visited the shrine with my grand mom. Did my life turnaround? You bet it did. I know it would be difficult to believe, as it may sound ridiculous, but that's why I said you need to experience Intuition to find out how it works.

Let me share with you another experience I have had with intuition. The network marketing business in which I was involved was not getting me any results, no matter what I did. For four years I kept asking myself, "How can I make it work? What can I do different? How will I be able to break free?" I kept asking myself again and again, and then I realized that I really liked to help people, and I was not pro-business. Therefore I would need to find a way of sharing my experiences with people who were seeking answers. Then I realized that I needed to write a book.

To elaborate even further, let me share another experience of mine. I always wanted to travel the world, so I kept applying for a job as a waiter on a passenger cruise ship for about six months. There was no reply, and I had almost given up on the idea. However, I then realized that I had been a disc jockey for seven years, so I gave it a final shot in the entertainment division because I had couple of strong references and loads of experience with technical aspects of the sound system setups. Guess what happened? I was employed, and I sailed around the world on a luxurious cruise ship for about two years—and I got paid for it!

You can also look at intuition as a light placed by God within us to guide us when we are seeking for answers. Intuition helps us make the right decisions we really cannot understand at the time of making them. An important factor that I have always considered during this process is to make God my reference point in regards to listening to my intuition; this really gives me the courage and hope that I need to move into the unknown.

Make God the Point of Reference

If God is for us, who can be against us? Romans 8:31

> "You always know which is the best road to follow, but you follow only the road that you have become accustomed to."—Paulo Coelho

How did I make God as my point of reference, and how you can do the same? I would like to explain with one of my experiences. When I was a disc jockey, I was interviewed on two music channels, and I had various write-ups on me and the club I was handling in major local newspapers, like *Times of India* and *Midday,* which listed me as one of the most popular disc jockeys of South Mumbai. I was made an offer to diversify into managing international music in music stores by a firm for their music store in Pune City, which is a couple of hours drive from my city, Mumbai. The fact was that I did want to diversify, but I had a challenge: my grand mom and dad had taken care of my younger brother, sister, and me. At that time (1999-2000) Grand mom was suffering from cancer, and Dad was unemployed and a cardiac patient. We had a legal fight for our property going on, and so as the eldest child, I had to choose between the new career and staying back and helping the family. I chose to stay back with my family and refused the offer.

I do not know where I would be now if I had made that choice to move to Pune, but one thing's for sure: I would not have been writing this book, and I would forever regret not standing with my family when they needed me the most. Making God as my reference point helped me to do the right thing. I knew from my previous experiences that being God-fearing helps me do the right thing and keeps me in God's protection; in the long run, it will all pan out. My choice was to simply trust God, let go, and let God. When people are young, it's not easy to think about God, right choices, and consequences—and to make such decisions. I am trying to point out a very important aspect of following intuition by taking God's ways into consideration, because no matter what religion people believe, there are a set of guidelines to follow and laws to abide by—that's why we have something called a conscience, to help us in this process.

The only way to understand and learn intuition is through experience: apply the learning and experience intuition; it's magical when we feel the light. The more that people experience intuition, the better they will be at understanding and seeing the unseen.

Ideas and Hunches

"The intuitive mind is a sacred gift and the rational mind is a faithful servant. We have created a society that honours the servant and has forgotten the gift."—Albert Einstein

Intuition, or the sixth sense, could also come to us in form of an idea or a hunch. When we have a clear and definite goal, and we are seeking answers or ways to accomplish the goal, we may get an idea or a hunch about how to go about achieving the goal. These hunches cross our minds in response to the questions we are asking and the answers we are seeking. As Henry Ford says, "If you think you can or you think you can't, either way you are right." Our mind is like a computer that runs according to the commands we feed it. If we command the mind to look for ways of how we can accomplish our goals, it will go on a search to find ways to achieve the goals, and vice versa. What we need to do is expect an answer to pop up at any time and take note of the ideas or hunches received; this is how we can anticipate opportunities that will be presented to us in order to help us achieve our goals.

I will share an example with you about ideas and hunches, and how it worked out for me. In the year 2005 I lost a big chunk of my home, we had to vacate the little bit of portion we were occupying in a few months and was desperately looking to buy an apartment in the vicinity of Mumbai. The loss of my shelter had forced me to have this goal, and I had no other choice but to buy my own apartment. Unfortunately the area in which I was looking to buy an apartment was out of my budget. The idea of renting an apartment crossed my mind, but I preferred ownership.

I started seeking for ways to buy my own apartment, and for a long time I didn't know how I was going to make it happen.

One day during a chat with a good friend at work, I learned that he was selling his apartment, which was in the outskirts of Mumbai, in Vasai, for a very small amount. It then struck me that I could easily afford an apartment if I looked on the outskirts of the city in Vasai, close to my friend's place. I began hunting for an apartment in Vasai but didn't like any of them. My father-in-law also owned a two-bedroom apartment in Vasai at the time, and finally after a long search I finalized an agreement for a beautiful, two-bedroom apartment next to my girlfriend's building. I hit a road block because I didn't have any cash to buy the apartment, and I didn't have much credibility to take a mortgage. After a lot of thought, it occurred to me that I had a few life insurance policies which I could leverage to secure the mortgage. My girlfriend then, Yolanda—who is now my wife— took a personal loan to pay the initial 15 per cent amount in cash for the purchase, and finally we bought our first apartment together without really spending a penny from our pockets.

In the process of buying the two-bedroom apartment, I grew personally, emotionally, and financially, and I learned many things. If I had not lost my house, I don't think I would have had the burning desire to look for an apartment, or the courage to take a mortgage. Losing my house proved to be a blessing because it automatically created a non-negotiable, definite goal for me, with a sense of urgency to act on it.

Create a definite goal for yourself, receive the ideas or hunches, act upon them, and improvise as you go along until you achieve the goal. Without a goal, you will not receive any ideas; you will need to send a command to your mind that you're seeking an idea, for you to receive it. A definite goal directs your mind to look for ideas to accomplish your goal; I will discuss goals and goal setting in the chapter on goals. Intuition is like a light within us, guiding us to make decisions. Through Intuition we will be revealed to the answers within us. The answers will not come overnight; we will need to keep asking, improvise on our questions if necessary, anticipate opportunities, and keep an open mind. Do not ignore the ideas you receive, no matter how ridiculous or absurd. When you are seeking, ignoring any idea is a lost opportunity. Take a serious note of the idea and make a plan of action, and all you need to do is act.

Passion

> "Belief consists in accepting the affirmations of the soul; unbelief, in denying them."—Ralph Waldo Emerson

"How do I know which idea will work?" My answer to this question is that I do not know. However, the last guiding factor that I follow in this regard is to follow my passion. How do I know what's my passion? For answers, refer to the section on know yourself. There are many quality questions left behind by successful people who have done this in the past.

- What would you attempt to do if you knew you could not fail?
- What is it that you love doing so much that you would pay to do it?
- What would you love to do so much that you would never feel like it is work?

- What would you do if you had all the money in the world?

Write down the answers to the above questions before you go any further. To the first question, my answer is to guide and inspire people to follow their purpose, which could be opening a restaurant, helping them find a better business that they may want to be involved in, or helping them to discover themselves. Let's take the second question now: what would I love to do so much that I would pay to do it? My answer is to educate myself and others through life coaching and motivational speaking; I want to help people to find their values. Let's take the third question: what would I like to do so much that I would never feel like it is work? The answer is to inspire, motivate, and help people, because I lose track of time in this activity. What would I rather do, if I had all the money in the world? I would love to educate and empower more people to follow their bliss. I drew my conclusions about my passion and came up with the idea of writing a book. Did it happen overnight? No, but it was a continuous process of curiosity that has led me here, and I am sharing it with you for your reference, to help you get your own answers. Did all my answers work in my favour? I'd say yes, because even if it did not it did guide me to the right place, it eventually provided me with the experiences I needed. Having a positive perspective always helps us find our way back, no matter how lost we may get.

> "Fascination is one step beyond interest. Interested people want to know if it works. Fascinated people want to learn how it works"
> —Jim Rohn.

I would like to share my experience with passion. I worked as a waiter for three years, and during that time I had developed a liking for music that I was exposed to while waiting at parties. After I had my first heartbreak, I decided to pursue music because it elevated me, and I joined a freelancing sound and music provider. I was still not very passionate about music—I just liked music. As I started playing for clubs, I started fanning my spark into a flame, and soon playing music became my passion. I could stand for hours without pain, play non-stop, lose track of time, and was completely focused. With this kind of passion, I naturally became good at playing recorded music; I could connect and feel the flow of the dance floor, which in turn got me a lot of recognition and coverage—and don't forget the money. Passion is needed in our work just like fire is needed for cooking. Passion can fan a tiny spark into a burning desire. Life is a great game of anticipation, and what you need to anticipate depends on who you want to be and what game you would like to play. It all starts with a tiny spark of desire to be and have, and when you fan this spark into a flame, you are set on fire. Let me share this small story I heard years ago with you with regards to how burning desires can work magic.

The Burning Desire

A young man asked Socrates the secret to success. Socrates told the young man to meet him near the river the next morning. They met. Socrates asked the young man to walk with him toward the river. When the water got up to their necks, Socrates took the young man by surprise and dunked him into the water. The boy struggled to get out, but Socrates was strong and kept him there until the boy started turning blue. Socrates pulled his head out of the water, and the first thing the young man did was to gasp and take a deep breath of air. Socrates asked, "What did you want the most when you were there?"

The boy replied, "Air."

Socrates said, "That is the secret to success. When you want success as badly as you wanted the air, then you will get it." There is no other secret.

Just like a small fire cannot give much heat, a weak desire cannot produce great results. If people have a weak desire, they will be indecisive and move back and forth, without achieving results, wasting the energy they are putting in their work. Getting frustrated and disconnected from their goals and finally giving up on them. A burning desire is the starting point of all accomplishment, a sense of urgency will help create the momentum and rhythm you will need to move faster towards accomplishing your goals.

FAITH AND BELIEF

"Take the first step in faith. You don't need to see
the whole staircase, just take the first step."
—Martin Luther King Jr.

You can read many books on success formulas, and you can
hear many inspirational speakers. They will speak about faith
and belief, because these two factors play an important role in
the accomplishment of your goals. I know for a fact that the path
to success in any endeavour consists of a certain set of rules, and
we cannot deviate from these rules no matter what. We need
these ingredients in the recipe of success. Let's understand what
these two words mean.

Faith

Faith has been used in all religious writings, and it has a great impact on our thinking ability. Faith simply means knowing that everything is going to be all right in the end, even though we don't know how at that point in time. Faith gives us a cushion of hope, which makes us feel the warmth in the cold; it makes us feel confident in uncertainty and empowers us with a positive perspective in every situation. As Kahlil Gibran said, "Faith is a knowledge within the heart, beyond the reach of proof." Usually when people speak about faith, they think of God, whom they cannot see. They have faith that someone is watching over them and will take care of things which are yet to come. In my earlier experience, I explained how, just with the goal of buying an apartment to have shelter, I took my first step in faith. As I advanced and faced challenges, the solutions always showed up in the form of the other decisions that I had to make and follow through. Faith is the antidote to fear and doubt. Faith gives people hope and confidence to move forward in the direction of their dreams. As Helen Keller said, "Faith is the strength by which a shattered world shall emerge into the light."

Faith is all about taking one step after the other through uncertainty. Faith can be in many forms: faith in God, in ourselves and our motives. But if we understand faith in God, it is all about the unseen and the unknown—and yet we have faith that everything will work out in our favour. Think about it for a moment: if what I experienced with the example of the apartment purchase is true, then do you understand what all of us are capable of accomplishing in life with this intangible yet solid, positive perspective? No wonder people like Mahatma Gandhi, Beethoven, Helen Keller, Thomas Edison, Albert Einstein, and many more accomplished great human achievements in the face of adversity, defied all common sense, and defined true success. To conclude, Edwin Louis noted, "Have faith in God; God has faith in you." Recollect your own experiences with faith. Look around you, how you notice babies having faith in their parents when they are tossed in the air, children learning to ride a cycle. All through life we have had faith at one time or the other. Faith is an invisible armour we must wear all the time.

Belief

> "Believe that life is worth living and your belief
> will help create the fact."—William James

Let's take a look at the word "belief", which people use in their daily life and yet are unable to understand its power. Faith is not yet proven, whereas belief is based on proven past experiences. Belief can be limiting or liberating, depending in which context we are using it. Our limiting beliefs are subject to constant change because of the progressive evolution we are experiencing. For example, would it be possible to believe that something as heavy as an airplane can fly in the air before the Wright brothers invented it? Would it be possible for people forty years back to believe that we could send mail across the globe within seconds, through email? These beliefs have changed and evolved as technology has evolved. Our beliefs are limited to the time and age we live in and are subject to constant change. It is very important to keep an open mind and keep up with the changing times.

Beliefs can liberate us when we use them positively to achieve our goals, for example believing that there is good side to everybody can keep us from fear, jealousy, hatred and mistrust in other people and save us time and emotional turmoil. Belief in ourselves, our abilities, and God can work wonders in our lives, just as we believe in the law of gravity and other natural laws, like the change in weather, or day turning into night. There are no doubts about these beliefs. Similarly, we will need to challenge our limiting beliefs and destroy them, moving in a state of faith and creating new beliefs based on new experiences. Our logic mainly operates from our belief system which determines what's possible for us to achieve and become for example if a person believes and creates a goal to retire at 60 with one million dollars in the bank account he will achieve it and become that kind of a person. However, if a person decides to financially retire at the age of forty he or she will create goals and become that person by achieving them. Understanding beliefs can either imprison us or liberate us, because beliefs are subject to constant changes as we experience new facts and evolve. For example when someone explains a better way of doing things like using social media to expand business and connections globally to a person who is opposed to believing in social media, it might offend them. Now this person has two choices either to defend his belief and imprison himself or accept and be open to change and learn from the expert on how to expand his or her business or connections globally. Psychologists will tell you that humans are all made of the same neurology, which in simple terms means what others can do, we can learn to do it as well, unless a person is genetically challenged as an individual in some areas.

The good news is that beliefs can be changed and upgraded to fit our need to accomplish our goals. How do we change and upgrade our belief system? There are many ways to do it, first you can start questioning your limiting beliefs which is causing you pain and frustration and ask yourself what's stopping you from changing the self sabotaging beliefs? Ask yourself is the pain of not changing much more then changing? What is the cost of not making the change as in where will you be in five, ten years on the current path? Make a list of people who have accomplished and are five years ahead of you in the new direction? Beliefs can also be changed faster through a point of reference and learning from their failures and accomplishments rather than doing things through trial and error. Let me explain with an example that really touched my heart: a story of breaking the world record in the Olympics taken from Wikipedia.

Sir Roger Gilbert Bannister, CBE (born 23 March 1929) is an English former athlete best known for running the first mile in less than 4 minutes.

In the 1952 Olympics in Helsinki, Bannister set a British record in the 1500 meters, but did not win the medal he expected. This humiliation strengthened his resolve to be the first 4-minute miler.

This was finally achieved on May 6th 1954 at Iffley Road Track in Oxford, with Chris Chataway and Chris Brasher providing the pacing. When the announcer declared "The time was three . . . ," the cheers of the crowd drowned-out the details of the result, which was 3 min 59.4 sec.

Bannister's record only lasted 46 days, and he was the first to admit that the 4-minute barrier had no actual significance. After Sir Roger Banister, many other athletes were able to run the mile within four minutes. Why were they not able to before? Simply because Sir Bannister had proved that it was possible, and others believed it, too.

With the example of Sir Roger Bannister, we can conclude that in order to believe what's possible for us, we may have to find someone who has already accomplished what we are working hard to achieve, and draw upon their experiences and beliefs. We have a choice to expand our belief system with what is possible by creating new, enriching experiences and by trying new things that challenge and excite us. Keep pushing your boundaries and expand your horizons to grow and create new sets of beliefs.

In my experience, when I was a waiter, that is what I believed I was. Until I decided to become a disc jockey, did I believe I could do it? Maybe, but I had a lot of faith because I knew I had the passion for music. I had accomplished becoming a successful disc jockey, spending seven years in the profession. I decided to move to the corporate world of call centres without any experience. I did not completely believe I could be a good customer service professional; I did have faith because I knew I could speak well, but I lacked patience and discipline, and I had to learn these qualities with training and practice I accomplished it. I moved on as a sailor to go around the world, and I had to learn what I needed to do in order to survive. Along the way, I created new experiences and expanded my horizons. My biggest fear was selling; I had to learn selling because I was in the network marketing business. I decided to move from customer service banking to the sales of banking products. It was risky, but I wanted to try and to learn. If I had to limit myself and stick to being a waiter—and not face my fears honestly—how far do you think I would have grown personally? By taking on new roles and challenges when required, I constantly challenged my beliefs and increased my learning. All I knew was that I had to do the things I needed to do in the given circumstances. I believe that if people are not open to changing and growing with the times, they will eventually find themselves stuck in a rut. To explain this further, I would like to share an interesting anecdote I read on limiting beliefs which we form because we may have failed before.

The Elephant Rope

As a man was passing by the elephants, he suddenly stopped, confused by the fact that these huge creatures were being held by only a small rope tied to their front leg—no chains, no cages. It was obvious that the elephants could, at any time, break away from their bonds, but for some reason, they did not.

He saw a trainer nearby and asked why these animals just stood there and made no attempt to get away. "Well," the trainer said, "when they are very young and much smaller, we use the same size rope to tie them, and at that age, it's enough to hold them. As they grow up, they are conditioned to believe they cannot break away. They believe the rope can still hold them, so they never try to break free."

The man was amazed. These animals could at any time break free from their bonds, but because they believed they couldn't, they were stuck right where they were.

Like the elephants, how many of us go through life hanging onto a belief that we cannot do something, simply because we failed at it once before?

The journey is completely mine and yours to experience, to live and enjoy the ups and downs in life. We all know that the only thing certain after birth is death. If this is true, what do you really have to fear, except for God? Being a beginner is an opportunity to learn and experience new things, and to grow personally, emotionally, and spiritually. The best way to understand belief is to see how a child learns to walk speak or learn anything new: it's like he did not believe he could do it, but when he sees his father and mother do it, he believes that he can do it, too. Thus children constantly change their beliefs as they grow up.

The challenge really starts when people are grown adults, and they choose a particular profession to practice or are forced to practice in order to make a living. How can a decision made at the age of eighteen by a person, followed without any questions up until he has turned sixty? That is more like self-imprisonment for almost forty years of a person's life. It's called conforming to what the society thinks is right for us, and we get conditioned to believe we cannot do anything else because we are taught to follow the norms. We have this one life, and we are meant to live in happiness, joy, and abundance. You are reading this book for a reason, because there are no coincidences. You have made a conscious choice to change your life and find yourself, and I wish you all the best in this adventure of yours. Our beliefs have brought us to where we are if we want to go further and pursue our dreams first we will need to change what we believe is possible.

SETTING GOALS

"Find a goal and focus on it like a laser beam,
until you achieve it."

Why set goals? Goals give us a direction. Setting goals is like setting a sail to our ship to reach a destination: a goal gives us a purpose to live for, to wake up every day with positive energy, knowing that we have things to do and accomplish each day—which makes life meaningful. Have you ever felt like life is meaningless, that you're stuck in routine, in a rut? Have you ever asked why people feel this way, why their energy levels are low, and why life is filled with one frustration after another for them? They feel this way because they may have no control over their life and where it is headed. Well, so the next question is why are some people happy all the time? Everything seems to work very well for them, and they have it all figured out and are happy. There are very few people who will constantly live in this state of mind. Have you met or seen these people around? What is it that these people are doing differently from others, to make them feel this way? Of course they also have problems, and they may be of bigger proportions, but they have the capability to deal with it with a smile. The question is what keeps them going? Even though some of them are not as smart as you are, the difference is mainly that they have found something many people are still looking for, or are still figuring out what to look for: a purpose and a direction.

> "Goals are not only absolutely necessary to motivate us. They are essential to really keep us alive."—Robert H. Schuller

Only you know what your goal is, what you want your life to mean or what you want to achieve is your vision and nobody else's—and it will always be different from others. Only you know deep down inside what you want, what makes you happy, and who you want to be five years from now. What is the meaning of life? Anything you want it to be, you have a choice. As C. S. Lewis pointed out, "You are never too old to set another goal or to dream a new dream." Goals, dreams, aspirations—call them what you want, but the fact is we all have it irrespective of where we come from, what we have, and whether or not we are educated. As long as we are breathing, life gives us the opportunity to be what we want to be, achieve or accomplish, and make our lives meaningful. Our goals don't have to big or brilliant to start with; all we need to do is sit and ask ourselves what our personal goals towards happiness are first; write our goals down for today, this week, and this month; make a to do list; organize; and plan. If you don't know how to go about it, make a list of things that you will need to do on a daily or a weekly basis that will make you happy.

It is as simple as that. I have learnt and realized that to begin with, our goals must be to be happy on a daily basis, with the activities we partake in. Slowly but surely we will be able to find our spark and ignite it into a burning desire. As the saying goes, a journey of a thousand miles begins with a single step. Begin with a simple goal: to just be happy daily. Is that so difficult?

Let me share the simple goals I found which were the key to my happiness. First, I wanted to be fit and healthy because I was underweight, and so I started working out. Second, I loved reading books because they nourished my soul and imparted knowledge; I believed that books had the answers I was looking for. No matter how bad things got in my life, I focused on my goals of exercising and reading. I would occasionally gift myself the books I felt I must read. As time went by, I started to be happier. With the knowledge I was gathering from books, I realized the importance of meditation, maintaining a journal, and spending time daydreaming of having things I wanted or picturing myself the way I wanted to be. As I went deeper in fulfilling these goals, I found my love for inspiring and motivating people through quotes. I started actively being a participant on Twitter, and soon I realized that the experience I had in life had given me a unique perspective to life; it was then that I decided to write. So far, so good: I hope I have been able to make my point here of beginning with simple things that make you happy on a daily or weekly basis, and maintaining a self-discipline week after week. Self-discipline will lead you from one clue to the other so that you move in the direction of living a more fulfilled, meaningful, and happier life. Right now, before you read any further, take the time to write down the things that, if you do them on a daily or weekly basis, will make you happy. Take control of your life and design your life rather than living it by default.

"If you go to work on your goals, your goals will go to work on you. If you go to work on your plan, plan will go to work on you. Whatever good things we build end up building us."—Jim Rohn

Process of Goal Setting

"If you want to live a happy life, tie it to a goal, not to people or things."—Albert Einstein.

Why goal setting? Now that you know the importance of goals, I would like to take it further and share with you the importance of goal setting. The process of goal setting is a creative process and is fun. Most people spend more time making a list to the supermarket than writing down goals that are really important to them; less than 10 per cent of the people in the world write down their goals daily. Writing down goals brings clarity and gives the mind a target. As the saying goes, "The future is a good place to be interested in, as we are going to spend the rest of our lives there." Our mind is like a heat-seeking missile, and its goals are its targets. Goal setting will allow us to figure out the minor and major steps that need to be taken in order to achieve our goals, and what changes will be required along the journey personally, professionally, and financially.

"If you don't know where you are going, you'll end up someplace else."—Yogi Berra

Goal setting is about laying the road map to arrive at a destination; it is like making a blueprint before you begin on a project. Daydreaming and fantasizing about achieving your goals starts the process of change, because the mind is directed in a particular direction, and goal setting helps you to control this change. Imagining your goals will enable you to visualize the events along your timeline weekly, monthly, three month, six month and one year that need to happen in a sequence on the way to achieving your goals. Goal setting will help you to align your values, life's purpose, passion, and the things that are important to you in harmony. In the first section, we have already discussed how to find your values, passion, life's purpose, and the list of things that are important to you. The process of goal setting will enable you to tap into your creativity and the child within you. Goal setting is the planning activity, which helps you visualize yourselves as you would like to be and create a path, carrying out activities with deadlines to reach; it's just like driving from point A to point B, point A being where you are today and point B being where you want to be five years from now, for now don't worry about how you will achieve it, just write them down the bigger the better, let your imagination run wild. The journey is far more important than achieving your goals, because during the journey you will be challenged to change personally, emotionally, physically, mentally, and spiritually. You will be challenged to perhaps unlearn what you have learned, or to come to believe what is true in simple terms. You will have to change and grow and bring about a new perspective to life, but that's the fun in the process.

Now that we have discussed and understood goals and the importance of goal setting, let's discuss the process of goal setting. If you study the lives of successful people, they have been through this process; because of the direction that goals have provided, they have achieved the seemingly impossible. Any goal can be accomplished if broken down into small tasks carried out daily. Goals have to be written down, just like planning; they can be short-term, midterm, and long-term goals. I would recommend that if you do not know your midterm or long-term goals then set your daily and weekly goals, which are short-term. If you can imagine your long-term goal even vividly, that's great; then you will need to set a deadline to it so that the mind is made aware of your target. Then work your goals backwards to yearly, monthly, weekly, and daily activities to reach your goals, breaking them into smaller and doable activities.

Let me help you understand this further. Let's say I want to finish this book with all the formalities and launch it in six months. I need to figure out, working backwards, how much of the book must be completed on a daily basis in order to launch my book on or before the deadline. I must be able to evaluate the progress on a daily basis, which will tell me how close I am to my goal and whether I am completing my tasks daily. I do this evaluation daily with the help of a tool called the sphere of silence, which is one hour of silent evaluation daily before I begin my day. You can use any method possible, and if you want to know more about using the sphere of silence tool, then you can buy Dato Sri Vijay Eswaran's book *In the Sphere of Silence*. This tool has really helped me control my day daily, rather than the day controlling me. I also spend time in meditation and daydreaming daily, where I visualize myself as I want to be when I have achieved my goals; this gives me great strength and energy to pursue my goals daily. I want to remind you that when you go to work on a plan, the plan also goes to work on you, which simply means that you may have to change certain habits which might not support your goals or might be slowing you down. Every time I faced this challenge, I simply asked myself, "What is better: to suffer now, or to suffer the regret later?" I knew one thing for sure: I didn't want to look back twenty years from now and say, "Hey, you know what? If only I had pushed myself, maybe I and my family would have had a better life." That thought always made me push myself harder, so that I could achieve my goals and grow into a better person while I was in the morning of my life. You need to look at your daily to-do list and compete with yourself to be better than yesterday; this will set the process of growth in motion.

Prioritize

Write down three of your most immediate and important goals. Write down the a list of five things that you would like to do in the week, or one step daily that will take you closer to your most immediate goal. Maintain certainty and clarity during goal setting, to prioritize and achieve your most important goal. Remember this is a process, and changes may happen under the light of new facts and circumstances. You should be flexible and open to feedback to adjust the course, which will lead you to the path you need to take. It's also important to note here that no goal is small or insignificant, because it has an emotional and mental fulfilment when accomplished. Therefore, list anything that's important to you. You will also need to consider the destination or the end result by asking yourself, "If I continue on this goal, where will I end up?" Answering these types of questions well in advance will help you get clarity about the goal, journey, and destination. Check whether it is okay for you to achieve your goal; your goal must be in alignment with your values and it must not violate the things that are important to you. I will explain this in the form of an old short story I heard years back.

The Midas Touch

We all know the story of the greedy king named Midas. He had a lot of gold, and the more he had the more he wanted. He stored all the gold in his vaults and used to spend time every day counting it. One day while he was counting, a stranger came from nowhere and said he would grant him a wish. The king was delighted and said, "I would like everything I touch to turn to gold." The stranger asked the king, "Are you sure?" The king replied, "Yes." So the stranger said, "Starting tomorrow morning with the sun rays, you will get the golden touch." The king thought he must be dreaming; this couldn't be true.

But the next day when he woke up, he touched the bed, his clothes, and everything turned to gold. He looked out of the window and saw his daughter playing in the garden. He decided to give her a surprise and thought she would be happy. But before he went to the garden, he decided to read a book. The moment he touched it, it turned into gold, and he couldn't read it. Then he sat to have breakfast, and the moment he touched the fruit and the glass of water, they turned to gold. He was getting hungry, and he said to himself, "I can't eat and drink gold." Just about that time, his daughter came running, and he hugged her and she turned into a gold statue. There were no more smiles left.

The king bowed his head and started crying. The stranger who gave the wish came again and asked the king if he was happy with his golden touch. The king said he was the most miserable man. The stranger asked, "What would you rather have, your food and loving daughter, or lumps of gold and her golden statue?" The king cried and asked for forgiveness. He said, "I will give up all my gold. Please give me my daughter back, because without her I have lost everything worth having." The stranger said to the king, "You have become wiser than before," and he reversed the spell. He got his daughter back in his arms, and the king learned a lesson that he never forget for the rest of his life.

The moral of the story is that if we pursue money as an end in itself, then we may be headed for disappointment. To avoid this confusion, ask yourself what you wish you would have done more of when you reach the end of your life? Write down the answers and make sure they are aligned with your goals.

Why?

After writing down these goals and prioritizing, ask yourself, why is this goal important to you? What will achieving this goal give or make you feel like? It is very important to know these answers before you can start working on your goals. Knowing what the value of a particular goal is to you gives you an edge and a personal attachment for that goal; when the going gets tough, this knowledge about your goal will be helpful in taking you through. Your goals can be small or big; as long as they make a difference in your and your family's life, they are important. If you are still not clear about your goals, it's all right, because it is a process; you will have to clear your head and your heart to be able to open up and tap into your true goals. Just go along and have faith that you will receive the answers and clarity when you are ready for it. In the meanwhile, keep going until you find new answers. Everybody has that one goal in their life for which he or she is ready to die for, that one goal that will define their existence and purpose in life, that one goal which will be their life's message, that one goal that, if they accomplish it, they can say that they has lived successfully, that one goal which will not allow them to sleep and they will pray and eagerly wait to go after it the next day. All you have to do is figure out what that goal or dream is for you, and the day you find it, you will be reborn and will become a new person with a mission. The more clarity, the better the vision will be, so keep digging within you. When someone goes digging for gold, they need to ignore the dirt and focus only on finding gold. People are born to a new existence and feel the heartbeat like music when they find their purpose in life; you will not get it overnight, and there is no fixed timeframe for you to find your life's purpose. All you have to do is move a bit closer daily, and when you are ready, it will be revealed to you. All the answers we seek are within us and will be revealed to us in God's time; all you need to do is have faith and patience.

"Be patient toward all that is unsolved in your heart and try to love the questions themselves, like locked rooms and like books that are now written in a very foreign tongue. Do not now seek the answers, which cannot be given you because you would not be able to live them. And the point is, to live everything. Live the questions now. Perhaps you will then gradually, without noticing it, live along some distant day into the answer."—Rainer Maria Rilke

Making God as the Point of Reference

It is important to make God a point of reference because it will keep us under God's protection and guidance, which is much needed when we are on the edge and trying to break free to achieve our goals. Making God a point of reference also gives us a cushion of stronger faith to strive forward during doubt, uncertainty, and breakdowns. Our conscience and heart must play an important role in striving for our goals, so that our success is long lived. We must be conscious about the steps we take in achieving our goals; to make sure we do not harm others or are not dependant on others to change for us to achieve our goals. We must follow our heart and be ethical. Remember, God loves everyone he has created, and when we choose to harm others for our purpose, which is acting from our freewill, we will reap what we sow (karma), and we will be far away from God's grace, guidance, and protection and may find it hard to find our way back. Think long term and think like a king or queen, a visionary whose work will carry on even after he or she is long gone. We must not compromise our values and principles for short-term gains because these will just be tests for us to overcome, and they will constantly tempt us to give in and take the easy way. Hold steadfast and ask for God's guidance. If we do stick to our values, principles, and ethics, then even if we do not achieve our goal through the current path, we should not worry, because God will open new doors and new paths for us and will certainly guide us to our destination. Every choice has its consequence.

I fought a legal battle for ten years with my tenants. The logical thing in the world would be to resort to violence and force, which was very tempting for me. But I knew somewhere in my heart that violence would only destroy and cause irreversible consequences. I didn't know what to do, but I made God as my reference point of view and decided against violence. I spoke to my family and decided to do away with the property, because that was not the battle we wanted to fight and be defined by. Besides, my family's safety was my biggest priority. I used my free will to save my family and leave in peace, promising myself in the presence of God that I would return back in the same vicinity with my family—and with a much bigger place—to redeem my family and me in God's glory. This dream has pushed me to take risks, be tolerant, come up with new ideas, and make difficult choices. I have failed again and again, I went through humiliation, and I almost gave up on myself, but I couldn't get my goal out of my mind, and then I had no other choice but to get up once again and fight to find a way and take chances. No matter what I do, I am always looking for ways to achieve this dream. As I mentioned earlier, our mind is like a heat-seeking missile, and it needs a target. Once it does have a target, it will not stop until it reaches its target. "If we protect our dreams, our dreams will protect us."

I know my mind won't let me have peace until I accomplish this. Did life tempt me with easy ways? Yes it did, but I have always been in God's protection and guidance because I am God fearing and believe in karma. God's protection and grace is very dear to me. I have experienced his grace, guidance, and protection, and I know as long I fear God and kneel before him, I don't have to fear anything on earth or bow before anyone else. I will not want to do away with it for any price, because I believe I will have what I want when I am ready for it, which is only dependent upon how hard I am ready to work on myself and my goals. In order to have what I want, I must first become capable of having it, otherwise how will I take care of it? I hope this makes sense to you. You are unique, and one of your goals could lead you to do a great deal of good work for mankind. Just imagine for a moment if Thomas Edison, Albert Einstein, Leonardo da Vinci, Mahatma Gandhi, Mother Teresa, or the Wright brothers had no goals. Where would mankind be today? It is your individual responsibility to have goals so that you can contribute your genius talents to the world.

Planning

"Failing to plan is planning to fail."—Benjamin Franklin.

The next process is planning, which is the process where you jot down steps to accomplish your goals in a defined timeframe period, working it backwards. This is the process where you can let your creativity take over, imagine, and write each and everything that comes to your mind in as much detail as possible, which can be collated at a later time with the given facts. This process is fun, and we can enjoy it because it lets our imagination run free. As Disraeli said, "Imagination rules the world." Write down what skills you will have to master. What are the new things that you will have to learn? List of people you want help from, to draw upon the experiences. Once you have put down all the points, you will need to consider the facts.

What are the things that will hold you back, or the obstacles that you will face in this journey? Every journey has obstacles, and you need to accept them beforehand. Imagining the scenario and the obstacles ahead gives you an edge to prepare for them and come up with solutions beforehand. Make a list of all the things that might get in the way, and then make a list of solutions to each one of the obstacles. For example, are you a slow learner? Do you not finish things? Do you have any habits that might get in the way? If there are inevitable obstacles, spend some time to think about how to handle them, and bring your focus back to the things that you can handle and solve; don't spend too much time on things that you cannot change or control.

Now that you have the goals, have prioritized them and checked if they are ethical, planned your daily tasks to get you closer to your goals, and made a list of obstacles and solutions, you can make a list of all the resources at your disposal that will be needed on a day to day basis to work your plan. It could be anything: an additional room, a laptop, Internet connection, a mobile phone, a car, daily expenses etc. When all these things are in place, go to work on your plan and build up on your daily small victories, because they will empower you to be better each day. Do not yet look at the results—just focus and maintain the daily discipline for a period of thirty days while evaluating each day with the to-do list completed. The purpose of which is to form a habit of completing the to-do list and getting better every day, which will then become a habit. Once you are habituated to small victories and to do better than the previous day, just like brushing your teeth, then you will be able to do it with much ease thereafter. Choose to focus on winning daily with yourself and build a winning momentum.

Network Marketing

Network marketing business plans are great for people who want to start with a minimal start-up in order to get the maximum return. People can commit and work for two hours a day on network marketing business and start generating substantial income, which can outperform any income a person can earn through a job. I recommend network marketing business to people who have no experience in business, because network marketing is a great platform to practically learn all about business. If people have a goal to be financially independent in about five to ten years, starting with a low risk and looking for high return along with lots of smart work, then I recommend network marketing to them. Network marketing business, which is based on an e-commerce concept, will allow people to build a global business, providing frequent travel opportunities to meet new people and have new experiences and learning the most important skill of dealing with people.

The three things to look for in joining a good network marketing company are as follows.

- Stability: How long the company has been in business; its credibility by its association with other companies; the company's vision and leadership.

- Training: People who have been working in a job and have never done business before will have to go through a paradigm shift from an employee's mindset to a businessman's mindset. The transition requires support through the team, support systems, events, training programs, and training materials. Training is a very important part of networking business.

- Exchange of product and service for money: Like any other business, a networking business requires a minimal amount to start, and the money is used for a purchase of a product or service in order to begin doing business with the company. It is important to do business with a network marketing company that exchanges products or services for money.

The company I did the networking business with is called QI Group of Companies, and the company is great. It has a great business plan, the training is the best in the industry, and so are the products and services. Their leadership and vision is inspiring. I learned a lot in the network marketing business, especially about how to deal with people and challenges, and how to be and think like a businessman, as it is a practical business school that promotes personal development, building relationships, training people, and being a leader. If people have not been to business school or cannot afford to go to business school, I recommend you start with a networking business just for the education, and to know what your own true potential is.

PART TWO

DECISION MAKING

"It does not take much strength to do things,
but it requires a great deal of strength to decide what to do."
—Elbert Hubbard

Once you have all the facts and a clarity in which direction
you need to steer, the only thing required is to make a decision.
Decision making is one of the most important skills in leadership
and life. Making decisions requires courage because once you
make a decision; you need to act on it with commitment.
Making a decision and acting on it is 50 per cent of the battle,
and the other 50 per cent is seeing the decision through. Action
taken without making a decision from within will be wishful
thinking. Decision making is also a continuous process because
one decision will lead to make many other decisions along the
way, and you will have to make changes along the way. When
you are faced with challenges, it's like a plane that may need to
change its course from time to time on its way to a destination,

so expect a setback and a detour, and also expect to find a new course of action around it.

I have met a lot of people who are not very good at decision making and therefore do not rely upon their own abilities to make one. The way to change this is to start making smaller decisions on a daily basis and committing to see it through. Smaller decisions made and seen through will start the process of self-reliance, self-respect, and confidence in your own decisions and commitments. When I work with people, I get them to make and see through small decisions. These decisions could be something as small as watching less television, making a daily to do list and completing it, or reading a book. This then sets the process of decision making in process. It is also important to once again remember that no decision stands in isolation, and therefore you will need to evaluate and understand your circumstances and keep improvising on your decisions as you go along. Another way to begin to start making decisions is to start making suggestions in a group.

In my experiences that I have already shared with you—whether it was to change my profession, buy an apartment, pursue my values, or align my goals—I have already made it clear how one decision leads to another, and all the dots get connected eventually when we look back. For example my simple decisions to become fit and healthy and reading books led to many other decisions that followed thereafter.

WORK ON THINGS YOU CAN CHANGE

"Start by doing what's necessary; then do what's possible;
and suddenly you are doing the impossible."
—Saint Francis of Assisi

When we make decisions to achieve big goals, the next task we need to take into consideration is the list of things within our control and outside our control. We cannot change things out of our control and have little or no effect upon them; however, looking at things we can change and starting to work on them will eventually give us the necessary momentum needed to have breakthroughs in its perfect timing. We will need to learn and experience that achieving big goals needs to be worked upon by breaking them down into smaller achievable goals, which we need to work on a daily basis. The first thing you can control and change is you: you are your biggest asset. Let me explain what I mean by this. Let's say we are headed to a far-off place, and we do not know how to get there because we have never been there before. We find out whatever information available at hand, and we also speak and take guidance from a person who has been there before us (a mentor). While we are travelling, we will look at how close we are on a daily basis, changing decisions when necessary, under the light of new circumstances. Once in a while, we think of the ultimate destination but focus daily on what our eyes can see and understand. It's simple when we break down bigger goals into smaller, doable tasks on a daily basis, by doing what is necessary. We have already set out to do the impossible, which is not yet visible and understood. As the mystery unfolds, the adventure gets more interesting. You also need to remember that you must be willing to change as you go along. As the saying goes, "When you start working on a plan, the plan goes to work on you." What you must understand is that you will change and grow into a new and a better person as you go along this journey. On this journey, your beliefs and point of view will keep changing in the light of new circumstances, and your character and emotions will be hammered and shaped as per the requirements to be a person who can have the capacity to achieve those bigger goals in life.

FOCUS

"The key to success is to focus your conscious mind
on things you desire not things you fear."
—Brian Tracy

"The world will be busy telling you and pointing out your
mistakes, it is your responsibility to look at the good in you and
focus on doing things that make you happy and feel great."

You may have heard of the saying that you always get
more of what you focus on. If you pass the sunlight through
a magnifying glass on a piece of paper long enough, the paper
will catch fire. When I focused, I understood how I operated in
life and in situations, and why I was not getting the results that
I was expecting. Let me explain this in simple terms. When you
look through a needle's eye, everything in its path and beyond
looks blurred; similarly, when you focus elsewhere, the needle's
eye will be blurred. It is safe to say that you will only see what

you focus on. Let's say you are sitting in a room, and I ask you to focus particularly on anything that is red in the room. Because of my instructions, your focus will look for anything that's red, and you will find many things coloured red while ignoring all other colours. Now, let's say I ask you to look for anything in green. When you shift your focus looking for green, you will not notice red but will seek to find anything in green. I hope you understand how our ability to focus works, and why we see more of certain things because we are seeking them. It is safe to say that if we are predominantly thinking negative thoughts, we will find more and more things to be negative about. Choose to focus on the positive and the things you want to do and have in life.

How did I use this practice in my life? Our mind is the biggest trickster we will ever know. When I actually understood about how we always get more of what we focus on, I learned how I could change my life around 360 degrees, and I learned I could use this ability in every aspect of my life. You see, my mind was by default programmed to focus on all the self-sabotaging patterns like fear, guilt, anger, victim mentality, irresponsibility, failures, and low self-image. Using the earlier examples of how focus works, I learned that I was focusing on all the things I did not want, and therefore I wasn't finding any positive results—my mind was wired the wrong way. I started to create more happy memories to focus on, to replace the old bad memories. I started focusing on solutions and things I could change, and started winning with myself on smaller tasks first. That gave me a great morale boost, and I started feeling good about myself and became more confident.

The mind, which is the biggest and most complex bio computer in the world, fought me daily because it was unconsciously wired to be lazy and self-sabotaging. It was a hard battle that I fought to take back control. The self-sabotaging patterns running in my mind were unconsciously and deeply placed, and I was trying to change the strong momentum in the opposite direction of happiness, self-respect, and success. It was tough because initially I had to put the brakes on an already powerful, downward momentum, to take it upward. It took a lot of strength and courage to change it around, and I did fail many times and moved again in the wrong direction. However, since I had experienced the good momentum, and I was determined to achieve my goals, backed by my burning desire. I took on the fight again until I felt the positive patterns in focus becoming a habit. It is important to note here that you can change your world by changing your focus. Look for the good in people and ignore the bad; as the saying goes, see the cup as half full.

Let me explain this further with a Anecdote which will explain how you find what you seek for, because in seeking, you focus and work your mind in a particular direction.

Good People

A Yiddish Folk Tale

An old man sat outside the walls of a great city. When travellers approached, they would ask the old man, "What kind of people live in this city?" The old man would answer, "What kind of people live in the place where you came from?" If the travellers answered, "Only bad people live in the place where he came from," the old man would reply, "Continue on; you will find only bad people here."

But if the travellers answered, "Good people live in the place where he came from," then the old man would say, "Enter, for here too, you will find only good people."

The moral of the story is that we always find more of what we focus on and look for. As it is said, we don't see the world as it is; we see the world as we are. Maintain a positive perspective—you must learn to focus on the positive in everything and everyone so that you can work with a successful attitude. It takes the same effort to focus on what's bad about a person or a situation as it takes to focus on what's good. If we choose to focus on the bad in people it will drain us of our energies and make us dependant on other people for our outcomes, which will lead us to stagnation, frustration, and confusion. The only person you can change is yourself.

Focus on all the good that has happened in your life. Look and spend more time on the good that is there in your life, and new opportunities will be revealed to you which you could not see before. Get rid of people and things that make you feel bad, that are negative or are dream stealers, if you can help it. If you don't have anything good to focus on in the present, remember how good you felt in your glorious moments in the past, and then create more great memories to focus on in every sphere of your life. Spend more time in meditation and prayer to take back control. Surround yourself with books, people, and things you want to learn from or improve upon personally and professionally, and focus your energy on your happiness and the life you want to live. Keep your focus on enjoying the journey rather than being attached to the outcome. Being attached to the outcome will take away the pleasure, joys and learning's of the journey. As Mahatma Gandhi said, "Be the change you want see in the world."

DISCIPLINE

"The best thing about the future is that it
comes one day at a time."
—Abraham Lincoln

Discipline is the most important habit to inculcate. Discipline is about doing a certain set of activities on a daily basis, and these activities are non-negotiable—for example, creating a to-do list at the beginning of the day and seeing it through, or at least better then compared to yesterday. As we keep meeting our targets daily, weekly, and monthly, we will experience small victories; this will help improve our confidence, self-respect, self-reliance, and self-belief. We will get better at decision making and start getting more clarity on what is our true potential. Discipline will help us form these healthy habits, replacing the old ones, and in turn we will become more productive and happier. If we really look and analyze the reasons why we are not able to achieve most of the things we want, we will notice that it's mainly because of the habits that we have formed during our lifetime. Habits are behaviours formed with repetition over a long period of time, which have now become a part of your unconscious behaviour pattern—or simply put, we got wired up in a wrong way. That's why discipline is painful as we begin a process of rewiring. As Thomas Edison said, "If we all did the things we are really capable of doing, we would literally astound ourselves."

The way we can rewire our unconscious patterns of behaviour is through replacing old and unproductive habits with productive new behaviour patterns through repetition, thus rewiring our patterns of behaviour and becoming the person we truly deserve and intend to become. It takes twenty-one days to form a new habit. If we can add even one positive habit per month, imagine what we can become and achieve in this lifetime. Start exercising your mind by taking control of your mental faculties. If you have a burning desire to be the person you want to be and have what you want to have, then the fight will be more of fun, because anything that's not fun becomes routine and mundane, so you will fail to do it with your heart. If you hold the point of view of fun and the burning desire of being the person you want to be, you will earn your own respect.

"You only live once, but if you do it right, once is enough."—Mae West

TIME

"Until you value yourself, you won't value your time.
Until you value your time you will not do anything with it."
—M Scott Peck

Time is our biggest asset; once spend, we cannot get it back. We must spend our time wisely with things and people we love to be around. In fact, our free time is our biggest asset, because the time we put into work is already compensated for. Spend this free time in learning and upgrading your knowledge in whatever you are interested in: develop a hobby, find your passion, develop your strengths, master skills and learn new things. Looking back, you will see and understand how much of your free time has been spent on doing things which did not make you happy or help you improve yourself. To understand time, you can also read the book *The Power of Now* by Eckhart Tolle; it is more of a spiritual book, but it has helped me understand myself in relation to time and how time is actually different from what we perceive or understand of it. All we need to do is live in the now, because even after five minutes it will still be now, so we literally only live in the now, and therefore we must always be completely present in the now. A lot of people are either living in the past or the future, and they do not enjoy the present because they are living in guilt, shame, and failure, which is in the past. Some people are always anxious and worried about the future.

Time is powerful and does not wait for anyone; what we sow is what we reap from time. Do you think it is wise to spend your free time wisely educating and upgrading yourself personally and professionally? Then in challenges and situations, your well-spent free time will help you; you will become your biggest ally and asset. In this ever changing world, everything is evolving quicker than ever before in history: something happens on one side of the world, and minutes later we can watch on television and the Internet around the world. Today before students can graduate and take up a job in the line of their studies, they will see that the software and systems they studied are outdated. The times have given rise to a number of different professions cropping up with every passing year, and if we do not take responsibility for ourselves and our families, we cannot expect the government, businesses, and bureaucrats to take care of us. In this time we see that we are all so well connected and yet so distanced more than ever before. We are on phones even at dinner tables with our loved ones, taking for granted the time we get to spend with them, giving lesser attention to their needs. We can hear, but we do not listen and feel what's been said. Love, compassion, and kindness have disappeared into the business of doing unimportant chores and running unnecessary errands. Jobs are demanding longer hours of work, and we have a lack of exercise and meaningful meetings with friends. We are evolving in technology faster than ever—and declining in humanity and the quality of life even more quickly. The laws of nature are the same for everyone, and they carry out with precision day in and day out, like the sun and moon. So is it with time. Free time well spent can improve the quality of our lives and that of our families. People spend more time learning to work the DVD player and making a list for the supermarket than they do learning to operate the most advanced bio computer: their brain. If people spent even a fraction of their time shaping their minds and bodies, they would live a more fulfilled, meaningful, and happier life.

PART THREE

MANAGE YOUR MIND AND EMOTIONS

"Your emotions are the slaves to your thoughts,
and you are the slave to your emotions."
—Elizabeth Gilbert

INSTINCTS

"The wise are instructed by reason, average minds by
experience, the stupid by necessity and the brute by instinct."
—Marcus Tullius Cicero

Instincts are more like a sixth sense and a part of intuition;
however, intuition is like the guiding light within, making
important decisions in the direction of your purpose. Instincts are
needed often to protect us from dangers, when we are challenged
on a daily basis. Instincts help us to use an appropriate reaction
in situations where we don't understand or see things clearly.
Instincts need to be trained so that we can become effortless in
using them, when we need them. It means we must use instincts
as often as possible, so that we can understand how they work
for us and how they don't. Instincts can be understood and
trained only with application, through trial and error. Instincts
mainly take over in difficult times, or times when we are lost or
confused, and we don't know what to do or which way to go.

Animals have instincts also, which helps them hunt or protect themselves. It will be very difficult to explain how instincts work, because they can only be experienced. Just like intuition, the more we use and correct them, the better we get at it, and the more these instincts get trained on trial and error, the more we learn to use them to work in our favour. Just like in order to excel at anything, we need to practice and train hard so that we can master a skill or an art—for example, learning martial arts. The only way to understand and train our instincts is through constantly challenging our limits, understandings, and beliefs in our respective line of work. Instinct cannot be understood or trained in our comfort zone of security, which is obvious because they will take over only when you are in danger and living on the edge. The truth is that everything has a price to be paid; any skill or art needs to practiced over and over again to be mastered. In my experience, if instincts are trained well and we understand intuition fairly well, then we can handle any situation with ease during chaos and in the face of adversity. Samuel Butler pointed out, "Life is like music; it must be composed by ear, feeling and instinct, not by rule."

When animals are hunted, and as they are running for their lives, how do they figure out which way to run or what is the best course of action for them in the heat of the moment? If someone tripped you, what happens? Your hands immediately work on reflexes and try and protect you from getting hurt. At that point do you consciously choose the course of action as you are out of control of the situation? I don't think so. You rely on your reflexes and instincts to protect you from getting hurt. How does our body know what to do in a situation like this? The answer is that it knows through instincts in these moments. Athletes and soldiers train for a long time before they get into action; their instincts are trained to compete and survive in their line of work. We humans have been gifted with many faculties to survive and endure; however, most of us are afraid to use these faculties because we fail to understand them—because we hardly use them or rely upon them. Just imagine if we never had fire drills in big buildings and offices, and there was fire. What would happen? There would be chaos because no one knows what to do or where to go in this situation. In life there are no drills; you can start training your instincts on smaller fronts like your day to day activities, or in your line of work. God has given us many gifts and resources, including survival instincts. People are looking for guarantees when they are afraid, but what they don't want to accept is that there are no guarantees. People will have to learn to count on themselves during adversity. We are hardly using a margin of our God-given talents, and therefore we do not exploit them and live up to our full potential. For us to train our instincts we need to be in action; only through the playing field can we train and develop instincts, like boxers in the boxing ring. Let me share an interesting short story I read about how everyone is looking for guarantees in life.

Before the young man began his studies, he wanted assurance from the Master.

"Can you teach me the goal of human life?"

"I cannot," replied the Master.

"Or at least its meaning?"

"I cannot."

"Can you indicate to me the nature of death and of life beyond the grave?"

"I cannot."

The young man walked away in scorn. The disciples were dismayed that their Master had been shown up in a poor light.

Said the Master soothingly, "Of what is it to comprehend life's nature and life's meaning, if you have never tasted it? I'd rather you eat your pudding than speculate on it."

This anecdote is true because if we want guarantees before we begin, how can we even begin? The only way to know and understand how something can be done is through trial and error. We cannot sit on the fence and speculate. Develop your instincts in your line of work through training yourself.

Develop Unconscious Competence and Enhance Your Instincts

Instincts are of unconscious competence in a given situation, because a reaction happens in split seconds. Whether it's riding a cycle or driving a car, we need to be unconsciously competent in the skill; it becomes a habit through consciously practicing it daily. Let's say, for example, I am learning to play a guitar. At first, while practicing I will need to be conscious about the notes, their order, and the position of my fingers to strum in a combination. However after a lot of practice, I become unconsciously competent and do not have to pay attention to the first challenges anymore; I know the order by the sound, and my fingers move on the fret smoothly. Knowing each and every position perfectly without being conscious, strumming, and singing along—this is an example of how you can train and develop skills unconsciously. Let's take my example of when I wanted to be a disc jockey. I did not understand how to mix and play two tracks at the same time. I did not know what song had what speed unless I started counting beats per minute and then accordingly picked another song with a slight difference, matching the pitches with a pitch control and then playing them together. I did not learn this immediately and did mess up big time while practicing and playing for a crowd. But as time went by, I got better and did not have to pay attention to the smaller details. Over a period of time I could mix two tracks within a span of five to ten seconds. With constant practice I had become unconsciously competent in the skill of mixing two songs, and that gave me the advantage to experiment more and get creative.

I will share another example with you. When I was in the network marketing business, the main activity involved talking to people, and that involved human interaction all the time. Sometimes it was very difficult for me to understand what was appropriate to say when someone passed a comment or asked an uncomfortable question with which I was not happy. Reacting was a challenge, and I would go back and reflect and write down on what would be a better response or course of action to handle a similar situation in the future. In the future, if a similar situation came up, I instinctively knew what I had to do or say. Similarly, whatever line of work you may be involved in or whatever skills you may want to learn and master, it is possible by applying it daily, reflecting, and correcting. It can make you unconsciously competent in the skills, which will in turn improve your instincts in difficult times. In order to be instinctive in a particular line of work, skill, or art, you must identify them and then create a game plan and execute it by keeping a daily record. Once you have learned to train and develop your skills on a daily basis in your life, you will eventually start training and developing instincts with ease on bigger things in life.

INSPIRE AND MOTIVATE YOURSELF

"Of course motivation is not permanent.
But then, neither is bathing;
but it is something you should do on a regular basis."
—Zig Ziglar

Make a list of your favourite quotations, stories, pictures, whatever inspires you. These items help you to move forward and keep you motivated. If possible, keep them right in front of you where you work so that it helps you to keep motivated. Motivation is the key to accomplishing your goals.

There are two types of motivations, internal and external. The motivation which comes from within will sustain longer than the motivation coming from the outside. When we are motivated to accomplish goals which will satisfy our values, and we have a burning desire to accomplish them—that would be internal motivation. Being motivated by a group meeting, support groups, or a story you read about somebody else's accomplishments is external motivation. Internal motivation is what will push us harder and help us sustain when the going gets tough: because the accomplishment will fulfil our values, we would be compelled to make that extra push which is necessary to break free. When we set out to pursue our goals, there are many things that will get in the way, the first being ourselves. Our doubts, our self-criticism, and our personal views and beliefs in our own capabilities (fear of being a loser, not being accepted, living up to other people's expectations, laziness, fear of success and a victim mentality) can sabotage any attempts to even begin the journey. Our burning desire to achieve our goals and live our values will push us beyond our current reality to create a future we want to have. In the end it is better to have tried then to have a regret right.

External motivation can be maintained by reading books, joining motivational groups on social networking sites, joining a support group sharing your values and interests, meeting and spending more time with mentors and like-minded people, and making a vision board or a dream journal to look at whenever we find ourselves in doubts and begin to wonder if we are on the right track. When we are lost and in doubt, looking at our dream journals and vision boards will calm us down, and a renewed sense of purpose will take over. Our mentors, support groups, and books can help us with their experiences and give us a fresh perspective to our situations, and we will learn what we need to do. Lou Holtz said, "It's not the load that breaks you down, it's the way you carry it." Your thoughts are within your control, and therefore what happens outside is secondary. If the thoughts you're thinking are not empowering and helping, change them and focus back on thoughts that will help and empower you.

Daydream

"Spend time daydreaming to design the ideal life
you want to have."

Set yourself a time to daydream daily, because daydreaming, and looking at ourselves in the future as successful and doing the things we want to do, and looking at ourselves as already being who we want to be can help us overcome any failures and strengthen our beliefs in our goals. Daydreaming daily empowers and renews our energies, and it directs us to achieve our goals. Whenever I have found myself low and unable to find the strength to get back up, I have always retreated in a quiet place, daydreaming about everything I want and need to be. It has always renewed my energy and sense of purpose, and I become immune to failure, rejection, and negativity.

Imagination

"Logic will get you from A to Z; imagination will
get you everywhere."—Albert Einstein

Daydreaming calls on the great gift of imagination. If you think you don't know how to imagine, just close your eyes and imagine your house, your office, your front door. We all have the ability to imagine. The greats of the past have and the present are using this creative faculty of the mind to formulate their ideas before they bring it to reality. All the ideas first begin in our imagination. Albert Einstein imagined the theory of relativity before he wrote it, and Walt Disney imagined Disneyland even before it came to existence. Imagination has no limits, and ideas received through imagination can be brought to reality. Pablo Picasso said, "Everything you can imagine is real." If you can see yourself successful, you will soon find an idea on how to become successful. Daydreaming is a state in which we see a reality we want to have, and we are free to imagine having it. Through imagination people make great movies, music, write stories etc. Just imagine our world without imagination, nothing would have been created.

> "Disneyland will never be completed. It will continue to grow as long as there is imagination left in the world."—Walt Disney Company

> "Anyone who lives within their means suffers from a lack of imagination."—Oscar Wilde

"All the money in the world is spent on feeling good." Ry Koodar With our imagination we can remove the middleman, money, and have the good feelings and be happy anyway. In our imagination we can be, own, and have anything we want, and we do not have to pay for it. For example, I can close my eyes and imagine having twenty million dollars in my account, and spend it in my imagination and feel good, happy, and rich. Wouldn't you feel happy if you had that much money in your account to spend? Of course you would. So what is stopping you? Your belief cannot digest the sum because it is far from reality, which is determined by your logic. Our imagination has no limits except for the ones we enforce on it. In order to have twenty million dollars in my account, I must first be able to accept it and imagine it, because if I can imagine it, I can receive ideas on how to earn it. In order for me to become who I want to be, I must first imagine being what I want to become and I will meet people and opportunities to help me get it.

> "Imagination is everything. It is the preview of
> life's coming attractions."—Albert Einstein

I want to ask you to stop reading the book for a bit and start daydreaming about how you want your future to be. You may not be able to do it for more than three to five minutes. All the doubts will creep in and tell you it is stupid to daydream, but if you can manage to imagine vividly of the person you want to be, and do things you want to do, you will forget about all your worries, which immediately puts you into a positive mindset. Do it regularly once a day, and you will become naturally positive and focused; nothing will seem to bother you, and you will have self-belief and will be happier than before. How much does it cost to daydream? For me it costs nothing but maybe five minutes of my twenty-four hours in a day. Is it worth it? Of course, if this gift makes me predominantly positive and happier without spending a penny, then it's worth every second of it. Using our imagination and daydreaming works like an antivirus for our minds and puts us in a position to focus on doing things that are necessary for our success. Our part is simple. Use this God-given gift as much as possible to steer us back from all doubts, opinions, negativity, and fears, to head back to a resourceful state of mind so that we can focus on what needs to be done and what can be done. Visualising our ideal future repetitively will become a part of our beliefs, just like in school when the teacher punished us to write a 100 times I will not make mischief in class.

As we become more positive, we will attract more positive situations and circumstances through the law of attraction, which will eventually make us happier people—and being happy is in itself a success in today's world, which is full of cynicism. You can start with any amount you are comfortable with spending in your imagination, and as you grow, so does your capacity to daydream. "There are no rules of architecture for a castle in the clouds," as G. K. Chesterton said. If you would like to understand how the law of attraction works, read the book *The Secret* by Rhonda Byrne, or get the DVD documentary and watch it again and again to understand it works; if possible, make notes, which you can refer to whenever necessary. Also read the book *Think and Grow Rich* by Napoleon Hill, if you would like to further increase your knowledge and understanding on this subject.

APPROVAL ADDICTION

"Look to God for what you need, not to people."
—Joyce Meyer

Everybody is affected by approval addiction to some extent or the other. Approval addiction is mainly caused by failures experienced and rejections in life, which create a false sense of insecurity and fear in us. As children we receive many messages from our families and friends; some are positive and some are negative. For example, some love us unconditionally and tell us how beautiful we are, whereas others reject us or call us stupid. Some friends love us and want to play with us, but others call us names and ignore us. This gives rise to approval addiction in us very early in life. Withdrawal of love and approval from parents as we grow up may make us tend to pay more attention to other people's opinions of us, and we could fall into the trap of insecurity leading to approval addiction. Children who have experienced any kind of lack in their personal lives growing up—

whether it is love, money, appreciation, or parental attention—generally may develop approval addiction.

I was raised by my grandmother and dad, and therefore I always felt the need for mother's love, which got me into the approval addiction trap. I grew up with a lack of financial support and with rationing of food, which added to my insecurities and fears—which kept me from believing in abundance. I also grew up without a sense of belonging, because we were not rich and I hardly had any friends. All these things had wired me up to become approval addicted, and I didn't even know it. After I read the book *Approval Addiction* by Joyce Meyer, it helped me realize how I was behaving around people and constantly seeking their approval, which always kept me on a hook with low self-esteem and hatred for myself. Now that I understood the problem, I needed a solution to rewire myself, and then I came across the book *I Can Make You Rich* by Paul McKenna, which included a self-hypnosis CD. By repetitively listening to the CD and practicing the exercises in the book, I rewired myself and changed my behaviour. To understand more about this topic, I recommend you read *Approval Addiction*; it's a great book to understand how approval addiction affects us, our relationships, and our lives in the long run. The addiction for love and friendship can affect our lives a great deal and hamper our chances of living a more fulfilling life. I was down and out in life and in business, and I did not understand why. That's when I read *Approval Addiction,* and then I realized the bondages that I was suffering from the addiction, and this realization helped me break free from them and pursue things that mattered.

Approvals that we seek are of many different kinds: acceptance of our decisions, love, understanding, and more. Our friends and families may not understand us completely because they cannot see the world through our eyes, and their judgments would be limited to their understanding and the way they perceive things. They may have never done the things we are attempting to do, and therefore they may never be able to understand. Don't get me wrong—I am not saying you should not consult or take advice from your loved ones. You should, because you will need them for moral support in your journey. I am simply suggesting listening to your heart and finding out what's the right thing to do. Besides our goals are driven from our desires and values, and therefore how can another person understand it? In the end I would like to say that life is a journey where we are allowed to make mistakes, and therefore we must make lots of them so that we can grow to our fullest potential and live life fully. As Oscar Wilde said, "Most people die of a sort of creeping common sense, and discover when it is too late that the only things one never regrets are one's mistakes."

Spend time discovering your own limitations so that you may learn to go beyond them. Step out of yourself and look at yourself objectively. Learn and understand more about yourself and all that you want from life. What does success mean to you? You are like a treasure that is seeking to be found. Be yourself because you are unique and have a purpose. Finding that purpose is your responsibility—make it your mission in life to find and live that purpose. The world needs your genius, contribution, and the talents with which you have been blessed. "We are not human beings having a spiritual experience, we are spiritual beings having a human experience." Pierre Teilhard de Chardin.

ASK EMPOWERING QUESTIONS

"To solve any problem, here are three questions to ask yourself:
First, what could I do? Second, what could I read?
And third, who could I ask?"
—Jim Rohn

"Life consists of questions and the art of living is learning
to ask the right questions."

We will either get the desired results for our efforts, or we won't. The way we talk to ourselves and the point of view we hold of the situation can either empower us or break us or further confuse us. The ability to empower or break us lies within our understanding and the quality of questions we ask ourselves about our situations, as well as the way we represent them in our minds. In an earlier section we discussed how we can use our mind to make us happy. In this topic we will discuss our internal dialogue, because the way we talk to ourselves will determine our state of mind, which in turn will make us stronger or weaker. For example, let's say you tried something, and it did not work out or turn out as you desired. What would you say to yourself? Would you say something like, "I knew I would fail. I am an idiot and am stupid. I can never do it correctly"? Now, listen carefully to these dialogues with yourself. Do you think you will be empowered by this conversation? Do you think talking to yourself like this is going to give you any empowering views of learning? In fact you're increasing your doubts and limiting your own belief.

> "I never learn anything talking. I only learn
> things when I ask questions."—Lou Holtz

If I ask myself, "Why do I always mess up?" what do you think will be the answer I get? "Because I am a loser and am stupid." Will these answers help me in a tough situation? Of course not, because the answers are not motivating and are disempowering. However, let's say I ask myself questions such as, "Well, it was not perfect, but how can I do it better the next time? How can it be done more effectively?" The answers to these questions will be empowering and will give me the feedback of the necessary changes I need to make to get the desired results and try doing it in a better way. This is what I mean by asking empowering questions, which will direct us to answers that will get us closer to our goals.

> "What others say to you is not important, what
> you say to yourself is." Lawrence Kinny.

Besides asking empowering questions, also the way we talk to ourselves on a day to day basis is important to maintain a positive direction and state of mind. When facing situations which we do not understand, and do not have within our control, we must avoid the trap of falling for criticism and flattery. As we are in pursuit of our goals there will be ups and downs and we have to accept them. We must learn to keep our own counsel while listening to everyone's advice, having faith that everything will turnout well in the end can empower us to move forward. Let me explain it with a small story.

Maybe

Once upon the time, there was an old farmer who had worked his crops for many years. One day his horse ran away. Upon hearing the news, his neighbours came to visit. "Such bad luck," they said sympathetically.

"Maybe," the farmer replied.

The next morning the horse returned, bringing with it three other wild horses. "How wonderful," the neighbours exclaimed.

"Maybe," replied the farmer.

The following day, his son tried to ride one of the untamed horses, was thrown, and broke his leg. The neighbours again came to offer their sympathy on his misfortune.

"Maybe," answered the farmer.

The day after, military officials came to the village to draft young men into the army. Seeing that the son's leg was broken, they passed him by. The neighbours congratulated the farmer on how well things had turned out.

"Maybe," said the farmer.

This is a very empowering story because it gives a point of view that everything happens for a reason, and the reason is always in our favour. With this attitude of trust in God's plan, it is easier for us to understand and look at life from an empowering point of view. If we really step back and understand the adversity, we can ask ourselves, "How does this help me?" The day we understand how to use adversity in our favour and learn from it, we will master the art of success. I am not suggesting that one should look at life only positively; spend time on things and situations that bother you, ask the right questions, decide on an appropriate response, and focus back on the tasks. Representing things positively only helps us to leave the things alone that we have no control over, while maintaining our focus on things that we can change and having faith that as the mystery unfolds, it will all fit in the plans God has for us.

MAINTAIN A SENSE OF HUMOUR

"Don't take life too seriously. You'll never get out of it alive."
—Elbert Hubbard

A sense of humour helps us lighten up and is good for laughter, which is the cheapest medicine available. It helps us take things in our stride and look at overwhelming situations and challenges in a funny way. A sense of humour will smoothly get us through unavoidable circumstances. People and leaders who are successful have bigger challenges then you and me, and how do you think they get by? They maintain a great sense of humour, no matter what the circumstances. Mahatma Gandhi said, "If I had no sense of humour, I would long ago have committed suicide." If we want to see it, there is always a funny angle to serious matters. If we cannot change something, then we might as well laugh about it, because being serious about it will only make it worse. It helps to laugh at our own mistakes because it immediately decreases the impact and makes it easier to handle our emotions. For example, if we get into a minor accident, instead of frowning and debating whose fault it was, what will happen if we smile at the other driver? The other driver smiles back, and it immediately changes the whole situation and makes it easier for both parties to endure.

"A person without a sense of humor is like a wagon without springs. It's jolted by every pebble on the road."—Henry Ward Beecher

PART FOUR

TAKE FEEDBACK AND IMPROVISE

"We cannot solve our problems with the
same level of thinking that created them."
—Albert Einstein

Feedback is important for us to learn and grow personally, professionally, spiritually, and even physically. Without feedback we will move heedlessly in a circle without making any real progress. Progress needs to be measured and analyzed in order to take corrective steps. Feedback will help us know whether or not we are on track.

READ THE SIGNS ALONG THE WAY

As you are going along in pursuit of your goals and facing each day with its twists and turns, you also need to learn to read the signs along the way. Your intuition and instincts will play an important role here. When we are confused and looking for ways to accomplish something, we do see the signs or opportunities that will help us along the way. However, we need to be seeking, focused, and observant. Many times I have read the signs along the way; sometimes I was right and sometimes I was wrong. Nonetheless, as I kept training my instincts to read signs, the more I read the signs and grabbed opportunities, the better I got. I believe that we can start reading signs in small ways to harness this gift that's been given to us—we simply have to pay close attention to our intuition or gut feelings. In order to understand reading signs further, I would advise you to read *The Alchemist* by Paulo Coelho; it is a brilliant fiction novel about a small boy's quest for treasure and the signs he has to read along the way. Also, watch the movie *Yes Man* starring Jim Carey. I am observant and can understand and see things beyond my eyes can see. After reading *Alchemist* I finally started understanding how to read the signs along the way. I read the book at least six times and started putting the pieces of the puzzle together to get a deeper understanding and meaning to my life. I understood my life looking at the past, gathering experiences and learning, and understanding how I could use them in the future.

I have been trying to read these signs ever since then. For anything that happens in my life, I try to step back from the situation and see how it helps me grow. How can I get out of the rut? What changes will I need to make in order to do better and get the desired results? I look at all the different angles of the situation, find out which is the apt one, and look for solutions: an adversity, a challenge, a new opportunity, meeting a friend or stranger. I am always anticipating signs through every experience and encounter as a sign of preparation to fulfil my life's purpose and reach my destiny. Signs and opportunities are all around us and are revealed to us when we start looking for them. If you need a friend, it's a sign to become a friend. If you have difficult people in your life, it's a sign to test your tolerance, values, and build your character. If you have a difficult situation, it's a sign to pray and ask for God's help, and to exercise your faith. If you want quality time with your family, it's a sign to do away with the unimportant tasks in life. If you want abundance, it's a sign to be happy in life and get rid of all the negative things and people in your life. If you want forgiveness, it's a sign that you need to forgive yourself and other people. The list can go on.

Let me share a few instances in my life where I have attempted to follow the signs. I fought a long, hard legal battle for ten years without any results, and I was financially and emotionally drained. There seemed to be no way out of this mess, so I kept asking myself what I needed to do next. I had no clue, and it was all dark with no light of hope. After searching for years, I finally realized that I had a choice in this difficult situation, and that surprised me because I had always had this choice but never realized that it was there. I could not see it before because I was not ready then. The choice was simple: I could continue with the fight and maybe salvage a piece of my property, but my family might fall apart, and the battle could easily take may be another five years; by then I would have no future, so I would lose another precious five years of my life. The second choice was let go of the property and save the family, and start building a family with a new future over the next five years, without having the property to worry or divide my family. I took the second choice and let go of our property, which according to any sensible person would be stupid. In my heart I knew I could either choose to fight the property battle, or the battle of life, and I found that the battle of life was my path. The first sign I got was to let go of the property, and the second was to secure my own home, which I mentioned in an earlier chapter: a two-bedroom apartment.

We need to have an open mind and be ready to detach ourselves from something we may care about too much, in order to follow the signs on our way to our destiny. The idea to buy a two-bedroom apartment in Vasai (the outskirts of Mumbai) came from a friend, during a conversation about the sale of his apartment. I got a sign to come to Dubai after my wife, Yolanda, got a job offer in UAE. When our first child, Daniel, was due, we needed a one-bedroom apartment on rent, and we rented the apartment. In the process we were introduced to the network marketing opportunity, and the sign to start a business came when I was looking to earn an additional income as Daniel was born. The sign to write a book came when I realized my values and purpose; I read an article about how Dr Deepak Chopra self-published his first book. I got the title for the book from a friend's T-shirt, when I was looking for my title. I can go on with many other examples.

If you are not sure of what signs you must follow, then write down your current mental, emotional, spiritual, and financial needs; align your values with them; and seek and anticipate signs or opportunities, whatever you may choose to call them. Remember to keep your heart, mind, eyes, and ears open. A sign could come from a phone call, a conversation, a request for help, an advertisement, a quarrel, adversity or loss, or while watching a movie. Anticipate and grab when you have a gut feeling or an intuition that you have received your sign.

Feedback from Failure

"Doing the same thing over and over again and expecting different results is called insanity."
—Albert Einstein.

When we are trying to accomplish something or are learning, we will need to occasionally pause and see the results. Just as when we are learning to ride a cycle or to play a guitar, we are bound to fail, and sometimes over and over again until we get it right. It can be discouraging, but we need to understand on what we need to improve. If a desired set of activities is not getting us any results, then we could move into a state called learned helplessness. Always remember that God answers to our prayers in three forms: "Yes", "Not yet", and "I have something better in mind for you". When faced with failure for a long time, we will need to reassess our approach, our values, and our heart. If we don't find our heart in what we are doing, we are just wasting our time and other people's time, and even if we achieve our goals, it will not make us any happier. As we are moving through the journey, we realize that the approach is violating our values and principles, and suddenly we might feel disconnected with our goals. Accept the truth and its limitation, because success is a state of mind where our work, and our values and our passion have to be in alignment. If these are in alignment, then we need to reassess our habits and our unconscious patterns of behaviour (which could be conflicting), making a list of all the habits we need to replace and the skills we need to master. Habits can only be replaced with more productive and empowering ones, as discussed earlier. Always remember that failure is not fatal, so don't beat yourself up; sometimes we need to fail in a particular endeavour because it's a preparation for the next one. Always believe that God is watching over you, and in the grand scheme of things, you fail from time to time in preparation to fulfil your destiny and purpose in life. When you do find your purpose in life, you will realize how brilliantly God has prepared you for success. The journey is the reward because who you become in the process of achieving your goals is far more important than achieving your goals. Let me share a beautiful short story I read that will help you understand this better.

P.U.S.H.

A man was sleeping at night in his cabin, when suddenly his room filled with light, and God appeared. The Lord told the man he had work for him to do and showed him a large rock in front of his cabin. The Lord explained that the man was to push against the rock with all his might.

So, this the man did, day after day.

For many years he toiled from sun up to sun down, his shoulders set squarely against the cold, massive surface of the unmoving rock, pushing with all of his might. Each night the man returned to his cabin sore and worn out, feeling that his whole day had been spent in vain.

Since the man was showing discouragement, the Adversary (Satan) decided to enter the picture by placing thoughts into the weary mind: "You have been pushing against that rock for a long time, and it hasn't moved." Thus, he gave the man the impression that the task was impossible and that he was a failure. These thoughts discouraged and disheartened the man.

Satan said, "Why kill yourself over this? Just put in your time, giving the minimum effort, and that will be good enough."

That's what the weary man planned to do, but he decided to make it a matter of prayer and to take his troubled thoughts to the Lord. "Lord," he said, "I have laboured long and hard in your service, putting all my strength to do that which you have asked. Yet, after all this time, I have not even budged that rock by half a millimetre. What is wrong? Why am I failing?"

The Lord responded compassionately, "My friend, when I asked you to serve me and you accepted, I told you that your task was to push against the rock with all of your strength, which you have done. Never once did I mention to you that I expected you to move it. Your task was to push. And now you come to me with your strength spent, thinking that you have failed. But is that really so? Look at yourself. Your arms are strong and muscled, your back sinewy and brown; your hands are callused from constant pressure, your legs have become massive and hard. Through opposition you have grown much, and your abilities now surpass that which you used to have. True, you haven't moved the rock. But your calling was to be obedient and to push and to exercise your faith and trust in My wisdom. That you have done. Now I, my friend, will move the rock."

At times, when you hear a word from God, you tend to use our own intellect to decipher what He wants, when actually what God wants is just a simple obedience and faith in Him. By all means, exercise the faith that moves mountains, but know that it is still God who moves mountains.

When everything seems to go wrong, just P.U.S.H.!

When the job gets you down . . . just P.U.S.H.!

When people don't react the way you think they should . . . just P.U.S.H!

When your money is gone and the bills are due . . . just P.U.S.H!

When people just don't understand you, just P.U.S.H.!

P = Pray

U = Until

S = Something

H = Happens

God works in miraculous ways, and just because we fail, that does not mean we cannot do something. Failure is also necessary for humility, and sometimes God uses failure to bring us to nothing and then to recreate us as he wants us to be, like a sculptor chipping away the pieces to give shape to a beautiful statue. Failure can teach us far more important things about ourselves than success can. As the saying goes, "Get lost and find yourself." Failure also shapes and strengthens our character, as Friedrich has said: "What does not kill us makes us stronger."

As you keep going from failure to failure, you keep getting stronger emotionally, mentally, and spiritually. Failure actually introduces us to our true selves because it forces us to get rid of the inessentials like anger, greed, ego, jealousy, pretence, and lies. Failure teaches us about what we should be attached to and what we must detach from. Failure only purifies us, just like gold is purified through intense fire before it can have any value. God is our goldsmith, and he will not let us burn and will pull us out of the intense fire when we are ready and have value. You will then do things from a different zone of existence. Failure is painful yet is necessary for God to chip off the unwanted things in our lives—like false friends, beliefs, and perceptions of reality—so that we can evolve to our full potential.

TAKE ADVERSITY AND TURN IT INTO AN OPPORTUNITY

Always remember you have a choice to react and choose your attitude. Mahatma Gandhi, Mother Teresa, Martin Luther King, and Nelson Mandela—what was it that they did different from the rest of the world? They took their humiliation, concern, and anger against injustice and poverty, and they turned it into their mission and their purpose in life, changing the course of history. They chose their attitudes and reactions differently, and they channelled their anger and energy into a life-changing mission, turning adversity into an opportunity that has shaped the world we live in today. We have the same choices these great people had; all we need to do is step back from the adversity or the challenge and ask ourselves how this can help us grow and what goals can we derive from these challenges. I am not talking about changing the world; I am talking about simple things like, "What will I have to become and do?" For example, a simple challenge of being unhappy will help you create new goals and plans to live a happier life.

As I look back now on the time I had my first heartbreak or rejection gave me a goal to prove my worth and substance, losing my house helped me create a goal for buying a new house, After the birth of my son I created the goal to be financially independent and with the realisation of values and passion I created a goal of making a difference. In the process of achieving my goals, I grew financially, emotionally, and personally. How did failure or rejection drive me on my path to become a disc Jockey? And time and time as the events unfolded I created new goals, which I would probably have never thought of accomplishing, and it brought me to where I am today. Adversity can teach us many lessons if we wish to learn from it; it can lead us into a positive or a negative direction, depending on the goals we create in adversity.

Adversities are also necessary for us so that we can get closer to God; it's an opportunity to pray for help and protection, and it gives God a chance to let us experience his grace. We don't remember God during our times of success and abundance, but mostly we take refuge in him in failure, humiliation, and solitude. By getting up every time I failed, I found it helpful to detach and ignore people's opinions of me, and who they thought I was or what I should do. I found the courage in failures to fall back on my knowledge, judgment, and imagination of what's possible for me. The more I depended on myself and my strengths, the lesser effect others had over me because they were never able to hold me down. I got to know myself better, and I knew that if no one was going to die, then it's worth a shot. I believe it is better to try than to regret in life, because regret is more painful.

Rephrasing and Reframing Situations

Rephrasing or reframing a bad situation that is totally out of control is the most empowering choice we can exercise. In the end, the choice to hold a point of view on anything we face in life ultimately lies with us. It is like we are holding a remote control, and we can switch to a desired channel anytime. If we can use this choice wisely, we can get through any failure or discomfort in life. What I mean by reframing or rephrasing is that no matter how bad a situation is, we must choose to look at it in a way that helps us, because if we hold a point of view that's against us, it can destroy our ability to deal with it. As the saying goes, "If you're going through hell, keep going." In order to keep going, we must learn to hold a point of view that empowers us. The intensity and the impact of a bad situation will depend upon the point of view we hold about it in our minds. Let me explain this with a couple of examples.

When Thomas Edison was asked how he felt about failing ten thousand times to create a light bulb, he responded by saying he had not failed once—he found out ten thousand ways it would not work. What do you think of this perspective? When the whole world was seeing him as a failure, how did he see his failure? It is clear that he chose to look at the situation in a way that empowered him.

Let's take another example. When a general was retreating from a battle and was asked why he was retreating, he replied, "We are not retreating—we are just moving forward in a different direction."

There are always two sides to a coin, and there are always more than two ways to look at any situation. This is the beauty of the choice to rephrase or reframe a view, to look positively at negative situations. What we choose to see will direct the results and how we feel, and so we can use our point of view to empower ourselves. Perception will affect how we react and feel about a situation; therefore just by shifting our perception to the one that will empower us, we will change the way we react and feel. Another great way of looking at situations that will empower us is to believe that everything happens for a reason, and the reason is always in our favour. Believe that it is part of the master plan of God's purpose for us. This puts us in a more empowering state of mind to carry on doing what needs to be done, believing that God will take care of the rest. Think about it for a moment, and look at your life from the last five to ten years. Try and understand how the big and small events in your life have unfolded and led you to where you are today. You can choose to look at it negatively or positively, and your reactions and feelings will depend on how you look at it. As you will put the pieces together of the past, you will then be able to handle your present more effectively and design your future.

Reframing and rephrasing will give us a new perspective and will help us see things in new light. We have the choice to turn anything negative into positive. Let me elaborate with a short story on the beauty of perspective.

> One day a father of a very wealthy family took his son on a trip to the country, with the firm purpose of showing his son how poor people live. They spent a couple of days and nights on the farm of what would be considered a very poor family.

On their return from their trip, the father asked his son, "How was the trip?"

"It was great, Dad."

"Did you see how poor people live?" the father asked.

"Oh yeah," said the son.

"So tell me, what you learned from the trip?" asked the father.

The son answered, "I saw that we have one dog and they had four. We have a pool that reaches to the middle of our garden, and they have a creek that has no end. We have imported lanterns in our garden, and they have the stars at night. Our patio reaches to the front yard, and they have the whole horizon. We have a small piece of land to live on, and they have fields that go beyond our sight. We have servants who serve us, but they serve others. We buy our food, but they grow theirs. We have walls around our property to protect us, but they have friends to protect them."

The boy's father was speechless.

Then his son added, "Thanks, Dad, for showing me how poor we are."

Isn't perspective a wonderful thing? It makes you wonder what would happen if we all gave thanks for everything we have, instead of worrying about what we don't have.

> "If you change the way you look at things, the things you look at change."—Wayne Dyer

Hope and Fear

Hope comes from a state of faith in our values, in God, in our beliefs, and in the goodness of others—whereas fear comes from a place of insecurity, anticipation of evil, self-centredness, and misunderstandings. We experience this battle of hope and fear within us on a daily basis, and this fight is continuous. Fear is what keeps us bonded, and hope starts setting us free. The world today survives on hope. "Hope is a waking dream," As Aristotle said. Fear paralyses us; as we fail to act, failure keeps building on us, and we lose our confidence, and start making excuses, and blame everyone else for our failures.

> "I find hope in the darkest of days, and focus in the brightest. I do not judge the universe."
> —Dalai Lama

Hope will help us to begin again and try one more time; we have hope because we wake up every morning. Fear leads to all kinds of negative emotions like worry, anger, jealousy, hatred, and mistrust, which break relationships and families. Fear in relationships increases and distances friends due to mistrust, misunderstanding, and suspicion; fear is ego.

"Fear makes strangers of people who would be friends."—Shirley MacLaine

Fear and hope are parts of us, and for one of them to be predominant, we need to dwell more on the one we choose, as we always get more of what we focus on. If we focus to dwell on fear, we will imagine our whole world falling apart because something went wrong, but may not in reality only in our imagination, so we start acting and behaving from the feelings created by the fear. If we choose to dwell on hope, we will immediately find faith and get a feeling that it is going to be all right in the end, and we are willing to try again. When the world says, "Give up," then Hope whispers, "Try it one more time." Hope strengthens and exercises faith, taking us closer to God's protection, and fear distances us from God because we are relying on our own understanding, which is totally limited, and we are paralyzed even before we can attempt anything.

"We must accept finite disappointment, but never lose infinite hope."—Martin Luther King Jr.

Hope versus Fear

- Hope says, "Try it." Fear says, "Are you sure? Because you're not good at it."
- Hope says, "You can do this." Fear says, "You can't do this because you have failed at it before."
- Hope says, "Take the leap of faith." Fear says, "Don't take the risk—people will laugh at you."

- Hope says, "You have all you need to make this work." Fear says, "You need more than you have to make this work."
- Hope says, "You have got to do something." Fear says, "Do not try anything new."
- Hope says, "Everything will be all right." Fear says, "Everything is ruined."
- Hope says, "Make new friends." Fear says, "Don't try, because you will get hurt again."
- Hope says, "You can learn." Fear says, "You will be humiliated and embarrassed if you try something new."
- Hope says, "Give them the benefit of doubt and build a bridge." Fear says, "They will destroy you—build a wall and stay safe."
- Hope will lift us. Fear will paralyze and destroy us.

Let me further explain how fear—which leads to anger, revenge, and bitterness—can sometimes consume us with this short tale.

Two Wolves

Native Cherokee Tale

A Native American grandfather was talking to his grandson about how he felt. He said, "I feel as if I have two wolves fighting in my heart. One wolf is the vengeful, angry, violent one. The other wolf is the loving, compassionate one."

The grandson asked him, "Which wolf will win the fight in your heart?"

The grandfather answered, "The one I feed."

I would like to emphasize that the thoughts and perceptions you choose to dwell and focus on will be the stronger ones and will be predominant in your behaviour and actions, because how you feel inside automatically reflects in your behaviour. Hope will develop more positive feelings and behaviour. The benefits of achieving this are tremendous.

> Our deepest fear is not that you are inadequate.
> Our deepest fear is that you are powerful beyond measure.
> It is our light, not our darkness that most frightens us.
> —Marianne Williamson

Fear can be of two kinds: one s of insecurity and failure, and the other is exactly the opposite, a fear of becoming successful and wealthy. We can sometimes also be afraid of becoming who we are meant to become, because we think we do not deserve success, and this fear keeps us from living to our fullest potential. Fear of success can be a reason of upbringing, self-destructive behaviour, habits, attitude towards learning, and relationships with money, others, and self. You will need to identify which one of the two fears is holding you back; in most cases it will be a combination of both. I definitely had fear of success and failure. I had fear of success because I was lazy, and my habits and priorities were all wrong; I had self-sabotaging patterns and behaviour because of approval addiction and low self-esteem. I had fear of failure because of a lack of belief in myself, a lack of clarity in thought process, and a lack of expertise available. I overcame my fears by working on myself using affirmations, meditations, workouts, and completing my to-do list.

I gave you some of the things responsible for my fears; now make a list of things that are holding you back. Accept your shortcomings, because nobody is perfect, and we are all a work in progress. Make a plan of action to convert your weaknesses into strength, break it down into smaller tasks, and begin to take action. It is a process and may take time, just like a baby usually takes nine months in the womb to form itself before being born in the world.

Fear is nothing but logic, which has limited knowledge of what it sees and understands, as opposed to hope, which goes beyond logic, mounts on faith, and sees and understands the unseen.

"He who has a why to live can bear almost anyhow."—Friedrich Nietzsche

I will now share how I have used hope and fear. I, too, have a constant battle daily with hope and fear, and I have trained myself to predominantly focus on hope. My thoughts are predominantly positive, and so are my actions, which in turn led to personal growth. When I decided to end my career as a disc jockey in 2001 after seven years, I was twenty-four years old and an undergraduate. I was afraid I was known in the business of music and clubs, but in the corporate world I was a nothing. To leave something well established and become a nothing again was scary. I did not know how I was going to be able to survive the change, but I chose to focus on hope that I would eventually learn and grow if I just decided to stick to the task at hand. Besides, I was led by intuition to change and had God by my side during this change. I failed miserably because I found it difficult to fit into a corporate culture. Fear did take over many times, and I was in the midst of a paradigm shift in the way I perceived everything. I had to become open to learning making myself vulnerable and an easy target.

> "Listen to your fears they are leading you to become the person you need to become."

Let me share another example, when I decided to move from being employed into business without a salary and cut off my bridges. I was terrified, but my previous experience with facing my fear had made me stronger, and I had faith in God and in myself. I chose who I want to become in the pursuit of my goals, so I knew I had to pay the price and took the leap of faith, hoping that I would accomplish my goals. Changes led me to being vulnerable and open to learning, and questioning my own beliefs led to doubts, low self-image, and loss in confidence. A couple of my own experiences that I have shared with you will tell you how I chose to face my fears and focus my thoughts on hope, because I wanted to achieve my goals to make my life meaningful, and the only choice I had was to do or die. Life is about taking on your fears head-on; the more fears we face and conquer, the more we will live out God's will and fulfil our purpose in life. Ultimately it's better to try and fail than to do nothing and regret, because the rewards and learning are in the attempt.

"A man who fears suffering is already suffering from what he fears."—Michel de Montaigne

Start small, face your fears, and make it a habit to focus on positivity and be empowered. Fear will rob you of your freedom and life—don't let that happen. Attempt and fail if possible, but try and not to regret; it's your life, and you have only one shot at it. When you choose to focus on hope, you will find God closer to you, and you will experience him and his grace. Don't miss the opportunity.

Self-Image

"The 'self-image' is the key to human personality and human behavior. Change the self-image and you change the personality and the behavior."
—Maxwell Maltz

Our self-image is about how we see ourselves in our minds. Self-image is very important in life because whatever we do in life will be the result of the self-image we believe to be true. There are people in this world who may not be very good looking, and yet people find them attractive. The reason behind this is that these people have a very positive self-image of themselves, and so they act and behave according to how they see themselves, not how they look on the outside; they feel beautiful inside out. Many psychologists have noted that plastic surgery can change the outlook of a person, but if their self-representation or self-image is poor, they will still remain unhappy because they are scarred on the inside. As we are growing up, some people send us positive messages, and some people send us negative messages. We start forming our self-image and we will never deviate from this self-representation in our behaviours and actions. We start forming this self-image very early in life; it is said children's brains are fully formed by the time they are five to seven years old, so we start forming our self-image depending on the messages, love, and care we receive from our families and friends.

> "The person we believe ourselves to be will always
> act in a manner consistent with our self image."
> Brain Tracy

Ask yourself how you see yourself in your mind. It is important because this will define how you see yourself, and the way you see yourself is how you are going to behave and act. Write down whatever comes to your mind, or you can also refer to the chapter. Know yourself; you will not be able to get clarity on this overnight because this is a process and has to be repeated until there is clarity. However, the good news is you don't have to wait to get clarity on who you think you are. I recommend that you buy and read the book *I Can Make You Rich* by Paul McKenna, and you will find faster and simpler processes to do in detail, to get your own answers. I recommend this book because I have used it and know the potential transformation that you can experience.

Sometimes when people have had too many failures, struggles, and negative influences, they develop low self-esteem and have a lack of self-belief; their self-image has been beaten down. To recover, one can start doing small things successfully daily and make enormous changes in self-esteem and self-belief, and eventually self-image. People can recreate themselves by developing a new self-image and live up to their full potential.

I shared earlier with you how I went through a depression. That depression affected me personally and my family as well, and I kept looking for a way to fix myself. Whenever I needed any answers, I would spend a lot of time in bookstores to find a book that could help me, and God always blessed me with one. There is a saying that whatever problems we may be facing, there is book written about it with solutions. I found the book *I Can Make You Rich* and bought it; it was with me for more than six months, and I had not even started reading it. When I was faced with the same challenges over and over again, I finally decided to read the book. As the saying goes, when the student is ready, the teacher appears. The book also had a hypnosis CD for meditation, and I started with the discipline of sphere of silence and meditating daily with the hypnosis CD. My life began to change slowly, and after about two or three months I began to notice my habits started changing. During the time I was depressed, I got wired up the wrong way. I kept following the discipline because I now knew the help I was getting from the self-hypnosis CD and the sphere of silence daily practice made me feel alive and confident. I soon started working out at the gym and eating healthy food, and I was now getting sharper and wiser. I could notice and feel the difference in my behaviour and thoughts, and I was amazed with my own abilities. I then started to make a daily to-do list for personal and professional goals, and I forced myself to maintain the discipline to meet my commitments. Soon my whole self-image was changing, building on my daily small victories with myself. That's how I was able to rewire my mind. I made a list of things to do with the family, and I did it; I spent more time with my kids, and it made me so happy. I felt like it was a miracle, and I never expected to change so much in such a short time. Ultimately the way I saw myself changed, and I now have a better self-image. My self-esteem and my self-belief improved, giving me clarity and direction towards my purpose in life.

> "Self-image sets the boundaries of individual accomplishment."—Maxwell Maltz

First start keeping promises to yourself and your loved ones. Make a to-do list and fulfil your daily commitment as much as possible. Get better every day and you will see your own possibilities clearly. You will see yourself as a capable person and your self-image will increase tremendously.

Do Not Compare Yourself with Others

> "The only person you need to be better than is yourself."

People have their own pace of growth in life because everyone is unique. Some are slow and some are fast. By comparing ourselves with others who are faster and better than us, we will be playing a different game rather than playing our own game. Comparing our growth to others around us can be de-motivating and bad for our self-esteem. We have to always remember that we have our own uniqueness and talents to bring to the world, to make it a better place, and therefore we must acknowledge and accept our own pace of growth to maintain peace and harmony within us.

I am a very slow learner, and I don't think that's my weakness—in fact, I think that it is my strength. Why do I say this? Let me explain it with a short story.

The Chinese Bamboo Tree

The growth pattern of this tree is remarkable. Plant a bamboo sprout in the ground, and for four or five years (sometimes much longer), nothing happens. You water and fertilize, water and fertilize over and over again, but you see no visible evidence that anything is happening. Nothing!

However, in approximately the fifth year things change dramatically. In a six-week period, the Chinese bamboo tree grows to a staggering ninety feet tall—that's right, ninety feet tall! Wikipedia suggests that the tree has been measured to grow 122 cm (48 inches) in a 24-hour period and can reach a maximum growth rate of 99 cm (39 inches) per hour for short periods of time.

It seems incredible that a plant that lies dormant for years can suddenly explode with growth, but it happens without fail with Chinese bamboo trees.

I see myself as the bamboo tree: because I am learning slowly, my growth is not yet visible on the outside, yet that does not mean that I am not growing. On the inside the growth is ongoing. In the right time when I am ready, the growth will be fast and appear outward.

"Competition is good, but competition with self is better."

Comparing our results with others will destroy our peace of mind and our capability to love, because we will be jealous and resent the success of the people around us, which will block the grace of God to flow through our lives. We will become unhappy and unproductive, we will lose all motivation to do productive work, we will accept failure, and we'll go into a state of learned helplessness. On the other hand, if we compete with ourselves, we will be less bothered with other people's success, and in fact we will seek help and learn from them, adding to our growth and relations. Allowing and asking for help from others in turn helps their self-esteem to grow, and it builds trust and friendship. Competing with ourselves will bring out our creativity and uniqueness in what we do.

Be Flexible

"Stay committed to your decisions but stay flexible in your approach."—Anthony Robbins

Sometimes things may not go as planned, and we may have to take a detour or change our plans due to certain personal limitations. In light of this, we must be flexible enough to change our approach in order to reach our destination. Flexibility in thinking, understanding, and approach gives us control over the challenge because we always have a choice. When sitting among people, notice that the most powerful person in the group will be the person who is more flexible simply because he or she has more choices compared to anyone else in the group, which means he or she has many ways of looking at a situation and therefore has more choices of responses. Whenever we are faced with a situation or a challenge, we need to step back and ask ourselves, "How does this help me?" Let me share a small, empowering story that will give you a new way at looking at situations, which explains why we must be flexible in our understandings.

Things Are Not Always as They Appear

There was once a man who was ship-wrecked and stranded on an island. Every day he prayed, asking God to send someone to rescue him, but to his disappointment no one ever came.

Months passed, and this man learned how to survive on the island. During this time, he accumulated things from the island and stored them in a hut that he constructed. One day after hunting for food and returning back to his hut, much to his dismay he saw that his hut was on fire along with everything else he owned! All of his possessions were going up in smoke! The only thing he had left were the clothes on his back. Initially he was in shock, and then he was consumed with anger and rage!

In his fury he threw a fist into the air and began cursing God and yelling. "God, how could you let this happen to me? I've been praying every day for months about being rescued, and no one has come, and now everything that I have is on fire! How could you do to this to me! Why did you let this happen?"

Later the man was on his hands and knees, weeping heavily, when he happened to look up and catch sight of a ship coming in his direction. The man was rescued, and as they were heading back to civilization the man asked the captain, "How were you able to find me?"

The captain responded, "We were voyaging across the ocean when we noticed on the horizon a column of smoke going up. We decided to go check it out, and when we did, that's when we found you!"

In life we are going to be confronted with challenges, problems, and adversities, and we can only grow through these. But keep in mind that what the devil has meant for bad, God can transform it into our good! What is a catastrophe can sometimes be a blessing in disguise. More choices lead to more flexibility, and more flexibility leads to more control on the outcome.

I will share with you a couple of instances showing how I have used it in my favour. The first thing is that I never get attached to my approaches, because I know that I am growing as a person on a daily basis. If I made a decision to achieve my goals after one year, I might just realize that I may need to change my approach. Many times I have come to dead ends, and I have kept going without results until I had clarity on how to move forward again, and which direction to move forward in.

I was a waiter for three years, a disc jockey for seven years, a customer service representative for seven years, a sailor for two years, and a network marketing businessman for nearly five years. I am detached from my approaches and am flexible to change them, because I believe it is God's will; I let go and let God. I believe God has been preparing me for something big based on my previous encounters with change, and how they have helped me. Flexibility makes me see situations and challenges as learning and growing experiences, because if I am not learning and growing, then life would be boring.

When we are not getting the desired results, then we need to eliminate ways and come up with ways to get the desired results. Having choices gives us flexibility to change our approach; being detached from approaches gives us choice to change them. As Richard Bach said, "Argue for your limitations, and sure enough they are yours."

If you find yourself confused or stuck at a dead end, look around, look within, and pray. Find out why you are stuck and ask yourself how it will help you. What are the options you have of moving forward? If you're still not sure, make a choice let go and let God. When you hit a dead end, the answer is always right there; hang on until you find the next clue. Be flexible always, because it will give you more control over the situation and outcomes. Look at situations from many points of view, and stay focused on personal growth and learning.

"Everybody is a genius. But if you judge a fish by its ability to climb a tree, it will live its whole life believing that it is stupid." Albert Einstein

PART FIVE

THE BATTLE WITHIN

THE JOURNEY

The journey is the reward in achieving our goals. What we become in the process of following our heart and our plans is far more important; it's better to become a person who deserves success in order to maintain it. It's like winning a lottery without knowing what to do with a lot of money: sooner or later we will end up losing the money, as opposed to being a person who earns the millions and will be able handle it better. Some people are in such a hurry to be successful that they work harder and faster without enjoying or learning from the journey, which goes against them in the long run. Allow me to explain this in a form of a short story.

Working Very Hard

A martial arts student went to his teacher and said earnestly, "I am devoted to studying your martial system. How long will it take me to master it?" The teacher's reply was casual. "Ten years." Impatiently the student answered, "But I want to master it faster than that. I will work very hard. I will practice every day, ten or more hours a day if I have to. How long will it take then?" The teacher thought for a moment. "Twenty years."

This small story reveals the importance of the journey, because if you're going to keep your eyes on the outcome, then how will you be able to enjoy and learn from the journey? Our evolution is a process, and it will happen when the time is right and we are ready to move to the next level. To understand more on this particular topic, I recommend you read the book *The Monk Who Sold His Ferrari* by Robin Sharma. It's a small book with great learning within it. I recommend books to you because these authors have been my teachers in my journey of becoming who I am today, and if you can read these books, you may be able to learn a lot of things that will eventually open your eyes to a whole new reality of life. Through these books I want to share and explain how I turned my life around, and how you can do it, too. I feel you are a person who is seeking, and therefore I am sharing the books that helped me. Your journey and evolutionary process will differ from mine; therefore go according to your intuition and instincts. I am simply laying guidelines that will help you discover your treasure faster than I did.

What Goes Around Comes Around (Karma)

I have learned from experience that what we sow is what we reap; this is a very important aspect of the journey, and we cannot afford to ignore karma. It is easy to be so involved in work and miss out on important factors that will help us sustain our long-term successes. Success today doesn't depend upon bank account balances alone; it depends mainly on the value we can offer our society and contribute towards making the world a better place. Every product or service is in demand because it creates a certain value in the society. I have experienced a constant rush in people to compete and make money faster, and because they are driven by this desire, they are willing to compromise on their values, principles, and conscience. Mother Nature has its own laws, and we are also governed by the same laws. If we sow the seeds for an apple tree, we cannot get oranges. This also stands true in the way we conduct our work and business on a daily basis. Like Mother Nature, we need to first give and work before we can receive. If we sow deceit, envy, greed, disrespect, arrogance, and misconduct, then what do you think we will reap? In the short run we may find success and enjoy the fame and glory, but when the time comes for reaping, we have to pay the price. In today's busy world, material success is counted in terms of money, fancy cars, big houses, and fat bank balances—not how one has gone about doing one's business in order to acquire it. Material success is transitory because we are spiritual beings and are just passing through life in a human form. I have seen people rise and fall equally fast. When we earn money for our work, that's a tangible compensation for our work, but what we forget to realize is that there is something intangible that comes along with that, in our homes. The money may get over sooner or later, but the karma or the seeds we have sown, which is the intangible part, also has to be reaped in this lifetime. The laws of nature are precise: sunrise, sunset, the weather. We can never run away from our karma; we will have to reap everything that we sow in this lifetime, and there are no exceptions to this law. For more on this topic, please refer to Dr Deepak Chopra's seven laws of spiritual success.

I believe that we must work ethically and bring in good karma. Earning a good karma is far better than earning a lot of money, because ultimately we are souls living in a body, and whatever we acquire in our lives, we will have to leave it behind. I believe that when God created man, he gave him free will so man could decide on how he led his own life—so that man may decide to pay the price for his own actions. God has nothing to do with the choices we make or what we bring upon ourselves; our free will allows us to decide that, and that's why God has given us a choice to follow our free will or his will. Following God's will is painful because it is full of trials and pains; he wants to shape our characters to take on his work in this lost world and fulfil our purpose for existing. We have to take responsibility for ourselves and bear the fruit of our deeds. I would like to share a simple story with you to explain how what goes around comes around.

What Goes Around Comes Around

One day a man saw an old lady stranded on the side of the road, but even in the dim light of day, he could see she needed help. He pulled up in front of her Mercedes and got out. His Pontiac was still sputtering when he approached her.

Even with the smile on his face, she was worried. No one had stopped to help for the last hour or so. Was he going to hurt her? He didn't look safe; he looked poor and hungry. He could see that she was frightened, standing out there in the cold. He knew how she felt. It was those chills which only fear can put in you. He said, "I'm here to help you, ma'am. Why don't you wait in the car where it's warm? By the way, my name is Bryan Anderson."

Well, all she had was a flat tire, but for an old lady, that was bad enough. Bryan crawled under the car looking for a place to put the jack, skinning his knuckles a time or two. Soon he was able to change the tire. But he had to get dirty, and his hands hurt.

As he was tightening up the lug nuts, she rolled down the window and began to talk to him. She told him that she was from St. Louis and was only passing through. She couldn't thank him enough for coming to her aid.

Bryan smiled as he closed her trunk. The lady asked how much she owed him. Any amount would have been all right with her; she already imagined all the awful things that could have happened had he not stopped. Bryan never thought twice about being paid. This was not a job to him. This was helping someone in need, and God knew there were plenty who had given him a hand in the past. He had lived his whole life that way, and it never occurred to him to act any other way.

He told her that if she really wanted to pay him back, the next time she saw someone who needed help, she could give that person the assistance they needed, and Bryan added, "And think of me."

He waited until she started her car and drove off. It had been a cold and depressing day, but he felt good as he headed for home, disappearing into the twilight.

A few miles down the road, the lady saw a small cafe. She went in to grab a bite to eat and take the chill off before she made the last leg of her trip home. It was a dingy-looking restaurant. Outside were two old gas pumps. The whole scene was unfamiliar to her. The waitress came over and brought a clean towel to wipe her wet hair. She had a sweet smile, one that even being on her feet for the whole day couldn't erase. The lady noticed the waitress was nearly eight months pregnant, but she never let the strain and aches change her attitude. The old lady wondered how someone who had so little could be so giving to a stranger. Then she remembered Bryan.

After the lady finished her meal, she paid with a hundred-dollar bill. The waitress quickly went to get change for her hundred-dollar bill, but the old lady had slipped right out the door. She was gone by the time the waitress came back. The waitress wondered where the lady could be. Then she noticed something written on the napkin.

There were tears in her eyes when she read what the lady wrote: "You don't owe me anything. I have been there too. Somebody once helped me out, the way I'm helping you. If you really want to pay me back, here is what you do: Do not let this chain of love end with you."

Under the napkin were four more hundred-dollar bills.

There were tables to clear, sugar bowls to fill, and people to serve, but the waitress made it through another day. That night when she got home from work and climbed into bed, she was thinking about the money and what the lady had written. How could the lady have known how much she and her husband needed it? With the baby due next month, it was going to be hard . . .

She knew how worried her husband was, and as he lay sleeping next to her, she gave him a soft kiss and whispered soft and low, "Everything's going to be all right. I love you, Bryan Anderson."

There is an old saying: "What goes around comes around."

Imagine for a moment if we give warm smiles, encouraging words, motivation, a helping hand, a friendly conversation, and appreciation—these small things to everyone we come in touch with daily. It can create a ripple effect that can potentially transform a neighbourhood, community, city, and even a country. Aren't we always asking for things from God? But someone asks from us, and we are reluctant to give it, so do we think God should give us what we ask for? The process of receiving begins by first giving. If we are stuck and need help desperately, we must immediately look for a person who is also stuck and looking for help, and help him or her; sure enough, we will find the solutions for our problems.

What we want to reap should be exactly what we must first sow it may not always give immediate benefits or gratification monetarily, but it will certainly take care of us in mysterious ways. When we were expecting our first child, Daniel, we wanted to rent out our own one-bedroom apartment, but we could not afford it. However, we did get a good deal after a long search, and it all worked out finally. Similarly, when we wanted to rent out a two-bedroom apartment, we searched and found a great apartment. Again we could not afford it, but we still went ahead, trusting God. My wife got an increase in her salary after we moved in to our new apartment, and we were able to sustain. For four years in the business, I hardly earned much income, yet I did help my other partners to earn more money than me, knowing well that God would provide in mysterious ways. God did provide, as my wife got another raise again, and we were able to see through that difficult period. God will take care of everything on the way; all God wants us to do is follow his plan for us as opposed to our plans for ourselves, because he knows what's best for us. Follow God's plan and let the mystery of life unfold, revealing its beauty and glory. I am in no way saying that money is bad; I have a family and two kids to provide for, and I do want them to have secure future and give them the best in life. However, I prefer to do it following God's plan and trusting that he will take care of everything, if I can continue doing my bit day after day.

We can either rely on our knowledge, which is limited or use our free will for our short-term success, or we can choose to rely on God's knowledge and protection by submitting to his will. We must give first whatever we wish to receive. Always remember that God is within us, because he has given us conscience and intuition to listen to ourselves so that we can do what is right and according to his will. Stay true to yourself, because life and situations will test you as you go along; as you are true to your values, principles, and conscience, you will develop strengths from struggles and a character for success.

Be Humble

Being humble requires a lot of strength because it always makes you look vulnerable, an easy target for someone. Humility is the highest form of self-esteem, because it means we are neither inferior nor superior to anyone. Being humble allows us to listen to other people's points of view, and to be open to learning to accommodate and adjust to their perceptions. Humility is not being a door mat to let people walk all over us; it simply means trying to understand things from other people's point of view. The moment we find the other person being arrogant, the choice to act calmly and be assertive still remains with us. Being humble is a difficult process because it constantly lets us think of giving the other person the benefit of doubt, and many people may and will take advantage of this for their own benefits. People who are humble are quiet, happy, and peaceful within themselves, and therefore they do not look for an approval from others. I have a constant battle with myself on this particular subject when things get unbearable and out of hand, but I have learned from experience that the more I try to be calm and humble, the more God is able to work through me for others. God's way is difficult to follow but easy to agree upon; the real challenge is whether we can implement it daily. In a competitive world where people are driven to succeed, ignoring ethics and its consequences, it's more like a jungle where people are willing to be successful at any cost. Some are hunters and some are hunted, and all people are waiting for an opportunity to do better than their competitors.

Humble people are assertive people and are not arrogant. There is a thin line between being assertive and arrogant. Being assertive means to stand up for what we believe in with all our heart, at the same time understanding that everyone has the same rights. Being arrogant means thinking that we are smarter and that what we know is the only truth. People who have been assertive and humble have led people to their way of thinking without force, simply by following their hearts and what they believed in. Mahatma Gandhi believed that freedom can be won without being violent, and he achieved it by getting people to his way of thinking, by being a living example and leading millions of Indians to join him not by force but by their own consent. Mother Teresa believed in humanitarian service of taking care of the less privileged, and she proved the same with her selfless service to people. Martin Luther King Jr. believed in ending the social injustice prevailing in society based on the colour of the skin and led his ministry to a historic revolution. There are many people who are still fighting today for what they believe in; I just mentioned a few of the famous ones. I believe that today, we as humans have the freedom to choose what we want to do in life. Humility is a must in every aspect of our lives today, because everyone wants to feel important, loved, and cared for. If we can understand this simple formula, we can and will make a difference in other people's lives. Companies and leaders from every field accept the importance of humility and its importance in everyone's lives, because today it's all about getting along with people. Let me share a small story on humility.

Practice Humility

Many years ago, a rider came across some soldiers who were trying to move a heavy log without success. The corporal was standing by as the men struggled. The rider asked the corporal why he wasn't helping. The corporal replied, "I am the corporal; I give orders." The rider dismounted, went up, and stood by the soldiers, and as they were lifting the log, he helped them. With his help, the log got moved. The rider quietly mounted his horse and went to the corporal and said, "The next time your men need help, send for the commander-in-chief." After he left, the corporal and his men found out that the rider was George Washington.

The message is pretty clear: success and humility go hand in hand. When others blow your horn, the sound goes farther.

Just think about it: simplicity and humility are two hallmarks of greatness.

Let me share with you how humility was important to me. As a disc jockey and young man, my attitude was always arrogant. My part of the job needed it, because in the competitive field of music, one has to believe one is the best in the business. With appearances all over the newspapers and television, I got a lot of fame and popularity, which in turn led me to further arrogance. God has strange ways of bringing us to our knees. When I decided to move to the corporate world, I was forced to choose customer service jobs in call centres. What did I have to learn? Let's see: I had to learn obedience and discipline, because it is important to the corporate world. I had to learn to talk to customers who were angry, swearing, and abusive, treating them with patience, empathy, and understanding. The customer service experience of seven years taught me the most important skill I have in me today: the skill of dealing with people. "Listening is a million-dollar skill, as everyone wants to be heard and nobody wants to listen." I could never learn this skill the way I learned it during my customer service experience; it automatically brought a lot of humility in my ways of dealing with people, and it taught me how to look at things from other people's points of view.

Be open to learning, it is the best way to be humble. Always remember you have not walked the path of the other person, so do not judge others—and besides, they may know something more than you. Maybe it's a language you do not speak, or they have mechanical skills you don't know. Every person who walks into our lives comes to us for a reason, and that's how I know God answers our prayers. As we fail to recognize these opportunities, we fail to learn and grow. If we have difficult people in our lives, they are there to sharpen us and make us better. Accept them and learn from them. Just like the knife has to be sharpened from time to time to fulfil its purpose, similarly other people sharpen us. Whenever I am dealing with difficult people, I tend to stay with them longer without trying to be like them, but just to sharpen and learn patience from them. If we believe that there is good and bad in everything and everyone, then I choose to look at the good side of the learning process, ignoring the parts that I do not want to learn. I believe that there are no coincidences in life; the people we like and dislike are like mirrors that tell us what we are and what we want to be like. Learn the good from them, taking into account your values and principles. It also works the other way. For example, you make a new friend. Remember he has moved into your life, and you have moved into his, to learn some and teach some. Being humble opens up a whole new perspective to the world, which has so much to offer to us, and we have so much to offer to the world around us. If you want to learn more on how humility will help you in getting along with people, read the book *How to Win Friends and Influence People* by Dale Carnegie. It's a brilliant book that can help you understand and deal with day-to-day situations with ease and clarity. I have personally read this book ten times, and I still continue to read it. Every time I read again, I learn something new in human relations and humility. Let me share this interesting piece I read about how whatever you need the most is always in your possession already, so be open to learning, and you will notice these miracles every day.

Everything I Needed

I asked for strength and
God gave me difficulties to make me strong.

I asked for wisdom and
God gave me problems to solve.

I asked for prosperity and
God gave me brawn and brains to work.

I asked for courage and
God gave me dangers to overcome.

I asked for patience and
God placed me in situations where I was forced
to wait.

I asked for love and
God gave me troubled people to help.

I asked for favors and
God gave me opportunities.

I received nothing I wanted.
I received everything I needed.

My prayers have all been answered.

Forgiveness

"Getting angry is natural; staying angry is a
choice."

Forgiveness is the key to having peace and control of emotions in chaos. Nobody is perfect, so we will be dealing with people on our way to accomplishing our goals, and we will get hurt and be hurt by the choices we make along the way. Therefore it is very important to learn forgiveness. Forgiveness in the world we live today is difficult simply because if we are the forgiving type, we will suffer the most. Everything has its drawbacks and opportunities, and I would like to discuss the opportunities with you. There are three aspects to forgiveness for me: forgiveness to yourself, forgiveness to or from the other person, and forgiveness from God.

Why forgive ourselves? Simply because we are humans and make bad judgments and bad calls sometimes. We get angry and say and do things we usually don't mean, thus creating bad feelings of regret and guilt. These feelings, if fed continuously, eat upon our happiness, hope, and peace of mind, and they make our fears stronger, which in turn will form within us a self-defeating pattern for any attempts to succeed and be happy. It is better to deal with these feelings as soon as possible before they slip into the unconscious behaviour pattern.

The first step is to accept that we hurt someone or we've been hurt. Acceptance begins the process of healing and forgiveness, whereas being in denial is running away from the truth and living in constant fear, and defending our fears makes it even worse because our fear will continue to feed on anger, resentment, guilt, ego, insecurity, and mistrust. We have to be brutally honest with ourselves when faced with such situations; without honesty, it is difficult to find a solution and move on—and as long as we do not resolve it, we cannot be free of it. These situations require closure, which is forgiveness, and forgiveness sets us free of these unnecessary bondages and makes it easier to move on.

All our negative feelings, if fed, will imprison us in our own egos, making us live in denial and defend our own imprisonments. By acceptance I mean our own acceptance of the truth within us. Our acceptance does not have to depend on other people's behaviour or asking for forgiveness. As I mentioned earlier, being free from this bondage is an individual choice, and we have to choose for ourselves and not for others. Our part is to take care of our individual truth; we can forgive ourselves by saying, "Okay, I will not do this in the future and will learn from the mistake." We can ask for forgiveness if there is a need to from the other person. Whether they forgives or not again is their personal choice, so let them exercise it, and ask for forgiveness from God.

This is what our duty is: to have peace and to be free from the bondage of fear, anger, guilt etc. I understand that it's not easy to forgive or to even ask for forgiveness; however, it is a great process and will set in action the healing process, if you allow it. If you think forgiveness is weakness, ask yourself this question: when we do not forgive, whether ourselves or the other person, how do we feel, and what are our predominant thoughts? Do we feel good and happy most of the time, or do we feel insecure and angry? Are we focusing our energies on accomplishing our goals, or are we using our focus and energies to put other people down by beating them through competition or mind games? Will we feel happy when others start doing better than us? Forgiveness is the attribute of the strong, because in order to forgive, we have to have a bigger heart to swallow pride and build bridges, instead of building walls. Forgiveness helps us quickly forget a bad situations and experiences that we associate with people involved.

Forgiveness sets us free from the control of the people who hurt us. When we don't feel anger or resentment towards the people who hurt us, how can they continue to have control over our emotions and mind? Forgiveness is a selfishly selfless act. If you ask me as I set myself free from the control of the people who hurt me, they can no longer trigger the same stressful response from me anymore; when I see them again, what they choose is their choice—I am only talking about my choice. If we do not forgive, then we must be angry and want revenge, or we will feel the need to defend ourselves, which will lead to hatred and jealousy and a self-imprisonment to these feelings. Do we really want bad feelings that will distract us from our goals? Don't we have more important goals to accomplish?

We are all sinners, and it is a fact and we do need and ask for forgiveness from God and people from time to time. Shouldn't we take the opportunity to forgive others? You remember what I mentioned in the earlier chapter: give first what you wish to receive. Besides, we do not know what other people's journeys have been in life, can we? Do we see the world through their eyes or understand the world through their understanding? I don't think so.

Prayers

"I have been driven many times upon my knees by the overwhelming conviction that I had nowhere else to go. My own wisdom and that of all about me seemed insufficient for that day."
—Abraham Lincoln

Prayer is a communion with God. Do we need it? If we do not have five or ten minutes in a day to sit in silence and pray to our creator, how can we have his guidance and protection? The further we are away from God, the more difficult it is to feel his grace. If we don't believe in God, it's okay; if we do believe in justice, goodness, peace, and happiness, that means we do believe in God somewhere.

> "If we are still asking, we haven't really learned to receive."

Prayer is not only about asking for things from God. For me, prayer is mainly to sit in silence and thank God for the beautiful things in my life, thus acknowledging his presence and grace. Prayer for me is to sit in silence, commune with God, feel him within my heart, and ask questions. The most powerful form of prayer is to pray for other people; anyone can pray for himself, but praying for others works best for all of us. In a prayer we need to have more heart than words—that is why praying in silence is the best way to pray. As Mahatma Gandhi said, "Prayer is not asking. It is a longing of the soul. It is daily admission of one's weakness. It is better in prayer to have a heart without words than words without a heart."

I mentioned in an earlier chapter that you should work on things that you can change, because if you pray and feel God's grace, then he will be working on things you cannot change, because he knows what's best for you. Prayers give us a certain sense of peace and security; though we cannot see it, we can feel it. Have you ever been distressed and troubled, and with just a short prayer, you felt good and regained peace and composure? I have many times.

"Do not pray for an easy life, pray for the strength to endure a difficult one."—Bruce Lee

It started very early for me in school. I had this habit of first visiting the church and praying to God and mother Mary before starting my day in school. Whenever I felt I was in trouble of not completing my homework or of being punished for any reason, I would say a short prayer to Mother Mary, and I would be saved not once or twice but every time. It was magical and unbelievable for me. It was and is still my magic mantra in troubles; even today I use it. Isn't it a blessing to have a prayer that will work for you when you're in trouble? That's how powerful prayers have been for me and I always end my prayers by saying 'Let your will be done'.

I have just shared with you why prayers are important to me, how they have helped me shape up, and how they have protected me. Do you need prayers? Ask yourself. Do you know what's best for you? Do you know everything you need to know about your situation? Do you have control over everything in life? Do you believe in goodness, equality, justice, freedom, and happiness? Do you have all the answers in life? Do you know what your purpose in life is, and do you need any divine guidance to find your purpose?

"Prayer is not asking. Prayer is putting oneself in the hands of God, at His disposition, and listening to His voice in the depth of our hearts."—Mother Teresa

Prayer is a very powerful way of having an honest conversation with God. Remember that no matter what our actions are, God knows our intentions, and we cannot lie to him. Prayer can also be in the form of questions and answers between God and you; when you ask God questions, the answer to these questions most of the time are found in the questions itself. Through the practice of sphere of silence, the last ten minutes is about writing down your questions for God. Read the book *Sphere of Silence* and understand how to use it. Let me explain this with a short piece I read about asking God honest questions and receiving the answers from the questions.

Questions

I asked God to take away my pain. God said, No. It is not for me to take away, but for you to give it up.

I asked God to make my handicapped child whole. God said, No. Her spirit was whole, her body was only temporary.

I asked God to grant me patience. God said, No. Patience is a by-product of tribulations. It isn't granted, it is earned.

I asked God to give me happiness. God said, No. I give you blessings. Happiness is up to you.

I asked God to spare me pain. God said, No. Suffering draws you apart from worldly cares and brings you closer to me.

I asked God to make my spirit grow. God said, No. You must grow on your own, but I will prune you to make you fruitful.

I asked for all things that I might enjoy life. God said, No. I will give you life so that you may enjoy all things.

I ask God to help me love others, as much as he loves me. God said, Ahh, finally you have the idea.

"Each one prays to God, according to his own light."—Mahatma Gandhi

Be yourself and pray according to your own heart and understanding of God and life. You don't need to be an expert or a religious person to pray. As you grow in a relationship with God, you will become enlightened and get better. If you are a person who does not believe in God, it's all right; just commune with the universe. There are many parallel beliefs like God, such as science and the universe. Choose with whom you want to commune.

Gratitude

"Acknowledging the good that you already have in your life is the foundation for all abundance."—Eckhart Tolle

Gratitude is the best attitude that can transform our life and can bring new meaning to life. It can instantly change our state of mind and give us a new perspective to life; it's a paradigm shift. Without gratitude for what we already have, we can never truly be happy no matter how much more we have in life. Gratitude is a state of mind where we learn to focus on our blessings, be grateful for them, and build on them. Want to know what to be grateful for? Just make a list of things you have that you are grateful for, and don't forget to list the things you take for granted, like this beautiful day, good health, family, friends, challenges, home, and family. Gratitude puts us in a happy state of mind, which in turn makes us optimistic because we begin to see the good in everything and are able to identify good opportunities in life. Isn't that wonderful? We always get more of what we focus on; imagine that with the blessing of simply shifting our attitude towards life, we can change our direction in life.

For example, let's say you wear blue shades. How will everything appear? Blue. Let's say now you wear orange shades. How will everything appear? Orange. Everything is still the same, so what changed is the way you look at things, through the shades you are wearing at any given time. If you wear the shades of gratitude and optimism, what will you see? Marcus Tullius Cicero said, "Gratitude is not only the greatest of virtues, but the parent of all others." That is why I said earlier that it is a paradigm shift and has the potential to change your life for the better. Isn't it amazing of how you can begin by being grateful, and you feel better and are able see everything as a learning opportunity?

"Gratitude can transform common days into thanksgivings, turn routine jobs into joy, and change ordinary opportunities into blessings."
—William Arthur Ward

To have an attitude of gratitude is a process; currently we may be wired mentally to focus on what's wrong in the world and in life, and to change that will require great effort on a daily basis, fighting with yourself to take control back from your mind. If the mind has control and is programmed in a particular way, it will fight you every step to retain its control. You will have to practice gratitude every day until it becomes an unconscious pattern of behaviour, just like brushing your teeth. In many cases the mind will give you reasons why being grateful is useless and waste of time. The mind is used to worrying and blaming, and you will not see results immediately because the results will take time to manifest through consistent daily self-discipline, focus, and conscious practice of gratitude.

"God gave you a gift of 86,400 seconds today. Have you used one to say thank you?"—William Arthur Ward

The fight is totally worth it. In the end, once we have changed the habit of worrying and blaming to gratitude and optimism, we will see the world in a more empowering way.

Smile

> "Every time you smile at someone, it is an action
> of love, a gift to that person, a beautiful thing."
> —Mother Teresa

The smile is universal language and is understood by all ages. You can begin the process of gratitude, and you will automatically find yourself smiling all the time. I have even managed to control my mind and smile when I am angry, because it makes me feel great. A smile will add value to your face and bring about smiles on the faces of all the people at whom you smile. A smile is very contagious and makes you look younger. For example, when someone cuts you off while driving, instead of honking, try smiling; it defuses the whole situation, and the person in the other car smiles back. A smile can enhance your value and put other people in a better state of mind, and it will help you increase your popularity. Thich Nhat Hanh said, "Sometimes your joy is the source of your smile, but sometimes your smile can be the source of your joy." Let me share this short story I read about the importance of smiling.

Smile

Mullah Nasruddin Inspirational Story

The Sultan of Arabia had grown very fond of Mulla Nasruddin and often took him along on his travels. Once, while on a journey, the royal caravan approached a small, nondescript town in the desert.

On a whim the Sultan said to the Mulla, "I wonder if people would know me in this small place. Let us stop my entourage here and enter the town on foot, and then you'll know if they can recognize me."

Accordingly, they dismounted and walked down the main road of the town. The Sultan was surprised to see that many people smiled at Nasruddin but ignored him completely.

Irritated and a trifle angry, he said, "I see that the people here know you, but they don't know me!"

"They don't know me either, Your Excellency," replied the Mulla.

"Then why did they smile at you only?" questioned the Sultan.

"Because I smiled at them," said Nasruddin, smiling.

We can then conclude how important a smile is, not only for you but also to the people around you. You can change a few things you do on a daily basis and thus end up changing people around you and lighten up the day for everyone you come in contact with.

Know yourself, and ask yourself what your unconscious pattern or habit of behaviour is. Is it that of worrying, pessimism, self-pity, and being a victim? The good news is you have the power to change it; if you want to change your unproductive habits badly enough, you will have to decide to take responsibility for yourself and be a more grateful and an empowered person. The choice is yours, and so is the path; only you can walk it and make a difference in your life and the others around you. The question is, do you want to be the change you wish to see in the world? If yes, then be grateful to God for the chance to grow and improve! Smiling is a great habit to inculcate all the time. Do you think if you smile all the time, your life will be better?

> "You'll find that life is still worthwhile, if you just smile."—Charles Chaplin

God-Fearing

> "We are not necessarily doubting that God will do the best for us; we are wondering how painful the best will turn out to be."—C. S. Lewis

> "With God in our hearts and love in our work, we have the power to make our lives a masterpiece."

Whatever we do with God in our hearts and minds, we are already blessed, so we need not worry about how things will turn out. We know that God is our light and our guidance, and we will be delivered to fulfil our purpose successfully. If we fear God, will we ever fear anybody or any outcome?

To me, being God-fearing has always been about making my decisions and choices, with God being my point of reference and sometimes letting God take control my life and see me through difficult times. Having God's fear in my heart is the surest way I know of to follow what God's plan is and to fulfil my purpose in life. I have been God-fearing since I was a child, as I mentioned earlier. I would pray every morning for protection in the church before starting school. Is it easy to follow God's plan? Should people rely on their intellect and understanding? If people are willing to surrender themselves to God and are willing to rely on his guidance, wisdom, and protection, can they be assured of deliverance? In my experience, I can vouch for it.

"Never be afraid to trust an unknown future to a known God."—Corrie ten Boom

Free Will versus God's Will

"Sir, my concern is not whether God is on our side; my greatest concern is to be on God's side, for God is always right."—Abraham Lincoln.

"Life is a test given to us on earth; temptations will test our will and courage."

We are a soul in a body and are just passing through this life. Our body is what we live in and we are not our body—we are the soul in the body. We do not own anything in this life, because we came with nothing and will leave with nothing. The only thing certain after birth is death, and the rest in between is a transition. We truly cannot be captured because the soul is free; one may capture our bodies but never the soul or our minds. Death merely is the transition of the soul returning back to its source after the completion of its purpose here on earth. The reason I wanted to share these thoughts with you is because if what I say is true, then the question is, why should we fear any test on earth? Why should we only focus on just building materialistic goals? I am not saying that it's wrong, but what I am saying is reiterating what a lot of wise people have said: that the love of money is evil and the cause of all unhappiness. We can choose to have materialistic goals as well as spiritual goals; however, if we love money and are attached to it, then we are blinded by our materialistic goals, so much so that we may pay no attention to our spiritual existence. Having God as a reference point will help us to keep in check with ourselves, and being God-fearing will make sure that we always maintain our balance. Free will is a beautiful gift given to mankind; we can choose to use our free will in line with God's will by being God-fearing, or we can use our free will to work with our intellect and logic and go further away from God. Sometimes people will also find conflict between free will and God's will, and this will confuse them regarding what is the right thing to do.

"Quit questioning God and start trusting Him!"—Joel Osteen

I see every opportunity as a God-sent opportunity. However, before committing to it, I take my time to see how it helps all the parties concerned. I then take the decision to go with the flow, because I believe everything happens for a reason, and there are lessons to be learned along the way even though I may not have all the answers when I begin. I don't judge anyone or anything; I just go with the flow.

"Coincidence is God's way of remaining anonymous."—Albert Einstein

When I was in business and was not getting any financial results for four long years, I started feeling a conflict within regarding whether I was on the right track. I found it difficult to understand what God's will was. I was confused and searching for answers because I was not enjoying doing the business anymore, which meant my heart was not in my work. Then later, I checked that my values were in conflict with what I was doing, and yet the business at that time was the only means to reach my dreams. However, I stayed in this confusion and the dilemma for maybe about a year, until I started getting some clarity. I realized my values were not being fulfilled. I was feeling negative most of the time because of no results, my heart was not in my work, and my health was suffering mentally and physically. At that point I realized that whatever is meant to be, will be. I let go of the business and took on my idea to write, knowing that God would show me the way. If I was meant to do the business, I would end up continuing it no matter what, and the business would pull me back. It was a huge leap of faith because I was putting my dreams on the line here. Thank God, my wife supported my decision, and with great courage and faith in God's grace, I took the step and wrote this book.

Let the first act of every morning be to make the following resolve for the day:

- I shall not fear anyone on Earth.
- I shall fear only God.
- I shall not bear ill will toward anyone.
- I shall not submit to injustice from anyone.

-   I shall conquer untruth by truth. And in resisting
    untruth, I shall put up with all suffering.

                                        —Mahatma Gandhi

It is necessary to have peace and God's grace through the trials? If you are able to understand and have all the answers before you begin, it would be easier to count on free will. God's grace flows through everyone's life; whether we are using our free will or God's will, the only difference is that we have to bear the consequences of the decisions and choices we make. Think long term and make your decisions. The question is, what would you rather have in the end: the consequences of being God-fearing, or not being God-fearing?

Honour your past

> "The past is the reason you have dreams and
> goals to accomplish."

If we look at our past—maybe five, ten, or twenty years back—and spend time on understanding the journey so far, we will realize the present and the future has a lot to do with what has happened in the past. We have evolved as a stronger, smarter, and wiser people today because of our past experiences and events, which have led us to where we are today and where we want to be tomorrow. The goals and dreams we have today for our tomorrows are affected and influenced by what was lost and gained. If we do not judge our past, only look at it as a journey, and try to make sense of it, then it will come together as the beautiful pieces of a jigsaw puzzle, and we will be able to make sense of today and create goals for tomorrow.

Let's discuss how the past influences the future. In past events, if we have felt pain and experienced adversity, and if we look at our dreams and goals for the future, they have to be related in some way. Our dreams and goals may be for fame, glory, and being loved by all; this is a general craving for all human beings, to be recognized and loved. However, if we dig deeper, the dreams or the goals of the future have been largely shaped by what we didn't have or have been denied in the past. We are where we are because it is meant to be. I hope this makes sense to you, because if you are able to make sense of what I have just said, then it will be easier for you to imagine and design your future and know your purpose.

In the year 2000 I found myself beaten down by legal, mental, emotional, and financial challenges, and I went through a depression. However, when all that was through in the year 2006, I got married and moved to Dubai. This was the start of my recovery process from my depression, and it was a hard battle with myself to get my life in control, because I had lost all sense of purpose. Looking back now, I can make sense of it: getting married, coming to Dubai, having children, getting into business, and then finally writing this book were all a part of the master plan. In this recovery period, what were my goals? The first was to take control of my life, because I had totally lost it. The second was to become healthy again, so that put me on a workout routine. The third was to replace my unproductive habits with productive ones. The fourth was to work on my self-image through meditation and self-discipline. The fifth was to buy a house in my home town, which I had lost, and therefore I got involved in a network marketing business. Looking at my life in the past, I understood my journey, and hence my purpose in life was to help others through their adversities. I know the "how" and can help anyone who has a strong "why" to recover and follow God's plan for them.

Twenty years back, I didn't know where I would be today, and twenty years from now, I have a fair idea of where I will be because I am much wiser and have more clarity now—however, it is subject to God's will. We must learn to look at our past in a way that it can propel us into the future, because you are unique, and your experiences are unique. If you are willing to look hard enough, you will eventually be able to come up with smaller goals that will lead you to your significant goals and finally to your purpose in life. Remember that small goals are not always about money; it could be to become healthy, to enjoy life, or to be happy. It's as simple as these ideas, and they can turn your life around. Let's expand on this further regarding how the struggles of the past are required to help us become who we are truly meant to be with a anecdote.

Struggle

A biology teacher was teaching his students how a caterpillar turned into a butterfly. He told the students that in the next couple of hours, the butterfly would struggle to come out of the cocoon. But no one should help the butterfly. Then he left.

The students were waiting, and it happened. The butterfly struggled to get out of the cocoon, and one of the students took pity on it and decided to help the butterfly out of the cocoon, against the advice of his teacher. He broke the cocoon to help the butterfly so it didn't have to struggle anymore. But shortly afterwards the butterfly died.

When the teacher returned, he was told what had happened. He explained to this student that by helping the butterfly, he had actually killed it because it is a law of nature that the struggle to come out of the cocoon actually helps develop and strengthen its wings. The boy had deprived the butterfly of its struggle, and the butterfly died.

Apply this same law of nature to our lives. Nothing worthwhile in life comes without a struggle. As parents we tend to hurt the ones we love most because we don't allow them to struggle to gain strength. Honour the struggles of the past and learn from them so that they can impart the wisdom you need to become who you must be.

Happiness;

"People are just as happy as they make up their minds to be."—Abraham Lincoln

Happiness is a state of mind and money is the medium to buy things that make us happy; however we can just remove the middleman and just be happy. Being happy puts you in a state of being alive; you can identify opportunities and at the same time make the most of the opportunities at hand. Also, being happy predominantly will make you a positive person, and no matter the situation, you will be in a self-empowering mode all the time. Putting happiness in work will create a positive momentum, which will bring about more happiness and fortune because what you get in life is dependent on what you focus on—so if you focus on happiness, what do you think you will get more of? Of course it is more opportunities to be happy. "Happiness is when what you think, what you say, and what you do are in harmony," as Mahatma Gandhi said. I know it is difficult to be happy all the time; however, the good news is that we have a choice, just like we have the right to vote: whether we exercise it or not, it's in our hands. If we didn't have a choice, then we would just be robots. The attitude we choose has the power to create or destroy.

> "True happiness is inside out and not the other way around."

Learn to live happily inside out, and not outside in. We must learn to be happy inside out, because then nothing that happens on the outside will affect our state of mind. When we choose to be happy on the inside, we are filled with peace and gratitude because we have no expectations from people or circumstances. The only way to make the most of life is to simply be happy, and that is the purpose of our lives. If you wish to begin with the simplest goal to change your life around, I suggest you make being happy daily a goal every morning.

- Happy to have a goal to be happy
- Happy to be healthy and alive today
- Happy to be me, one in billions
- Happy to have twenty-four hours today to do something worthwhile
- Happy to have the freedom and the ability to choose
- Happy to be a spiritual being so that worldly attachments don't matter

- Happy to have challenges so that I can evolve, grow, and serve my purpose

  "It isn't what you have or who you are or where you are or what you are doing that makes you happy or unhappy. It is what you think about it."—Dale Carnegie

If every day we wake up and affirm a simple goal of being happy for the day, every day for the rest of our lives, then we can start a positive ripple effect. It is a simple goal and yet a difficult one, because we have associated happiness with having a lot of money and material things. There is nothing wrong with having materialistic things, but the good news is we don't need to wait to have materialistic things in order to start being happy. We have a choice to simply be happy.

  "Learn to value yourself, which means: fight for your happiness."—Ayn Rand

If you really choose to look at the glass half full, you will find out how easy it is to be happy and content in smaller things in your life, like having an ice cream, enjoying cup of tea or coffee, enjoying the sunshine (and rain and snow), celebrating life, and capturing each happy moment in life as you go on living. As we choose to practice being happy inside out on a daily basis, we will then be able to influence and replace our unhappy habits at an unconscious level, and we will be predominantly happy. As we focus more on things to be happy about each day, we will discover more and more reasons to be happy, eventually making us predominantly happy. Remember the ripple effect: how do you think people around you will feel? Do you think they will be happier, too? By changing the way you look at things, you will be able to transform yourself and the people around you.

For the longest time I was unhappy and had predominantly become an unhappy person, because our human mind works with association and with the pictures we make in our minds with our thoughts. I was mainly focusing on the unhappy thoughts and pictures in my mind, and it had become my predominant nature, thus making my self-image destructive. Therefore I would feel unhappy most of the time, not realizing that I had the power to change what I was focusing on. I realized that I had made it a habit of being unhappy, that I was a slave to my mind, and that somehow I felt it safe to always remain as a victim because I was afraid of taking responsibility of myself. In short, I was afraid of my own success.

The mind is a powerful tool or a terrible master. Either you use your mind, or it uses you. Have you ever felt like attempting to do something out of the ordinary or taking a risk? What happens? You immediately feel fear, and the logical mind starts highlighting doubts and all the logic regarding why it is ridiculous to attempt to execute your idea and the reasons it will fail. Now you can understand what's happening here: the mind is afraid of change, responsibility, and hard work, and it wants to control you. If you still manage to decide to go ahead, the mind will fight you, and it will fight hard to take back control. When I realized this, I immediately decided to get rid of all the things that were negatively affecting my thinking and behaviour, so that I could create more space for positive behaviour patterns. To do this, I started being more observant of the beauty around me, focusing on smiling all the time, spending more time playing, and enjoying doing small things with my family, like a swim, brunch, holiday outings, working out, healthy diet, meditating, and visualizing the person I wanted to be. In the next few months I started taking control back from my mind. I had to fight with my mind daily, I still do, because this is a constant battle day in and day out.

> "Success is getting what you want; happiness is wanting what you get"—W. P. Kinsella

Whatever I have shared with you sounds very good in theory and makes sense to you, the reader. However, the success of this will only be sealed and signed by that one burning desire that you want to accomplish, that will drive you daily to carry this change without seeing results for some time. You have to find that one reason that will make this change a do-or-die situation. Ask yourself why you want to be a happier, content, responsible, and a successful person? Remember that being happy and content is truly the beginning of being successful. A lot of people have everything—money, material things, fame, luxury—and yet it is never enough for them. I am not judging them, because that is what they choose, if you become a more content and happy person with all that you have, you will create space for more, and yet have peace of mind and heart because your happiness will be detached from outside things. You will be a person who is happy inside out.

Success

> "A man is a success if he gets up in the morning
> and gets to bed at night, and in between he does
> what he wants to do."—Bob Dylan

Success is relative, and its meaning changes from person to person. Some people think of success as having a lot of money, and some think of success as having love and peace in life. For many others, success is about living life to the fullest and on their own terms, with lots of time and money. I would like to share a short story that will explain the essence of success.

Love, Wealth, and Success

A woman came out of her house and saw three old men with long white beards sitting in her front yard. She did not recognize them. She said, "I don't think I know you, but you must be hungry. Please come in and have something to eat."

"Is the man of the house home?" they asked.

"No", she said. "He's out."

"Then we cannot come in," they replied.

In the evening when her husband came home, she told him what had happened. "Go tell them I am home and invite them in," he said.

The woman went out and invited the men in. "We do not go into a house together," they replied.

"Why is that?" she wanted to know.

One of the old men explained. "His name is wealth," he said, pointing to one of his friends, and he pointed to another one, "He is Success, and I am Love." Then he added, "Now go in and discuss with your husband which one of us you want in your home."

The woman went in and told her husband what was said. Her husband was overjoyed. "How nice!" he said. "Since that is the case, let us invite Wealth. Let him come and fill our home with wealth!"

His wife disagreed. "My dear, why don't you invite Success?"

Their daughter-in-law was listening from the other corner of the house. She jumped in with her own suggestion: "Would it not be better to invite Love? Our home will then be filled with love!"

"Let us heed our daughter-in-law's advice," said the husband to his wife. "Go out and invite Love to be our guest."

The woman went out and asked the three old men, "Which one of you is Love? Please come in and be our guest." Love got up and started walking toward the house. The other two also got up and followed him.

Surprised, the lady asked Wealth and Success, "I only invited Love. Why are you coming in?"

The old men replied together, "If you had invited wealth or Success, the other two of us would've stayed out, but since you invited Love, wherever he goes, we go with him. Wherever there is Love, there is also Wealth and Success!"

What I want you to understand from this short story is that true success comes from doing what we love. If love is the core of all activities of our lives, we will work relentlessly and be truly able to make a lasting difference in our world. Success for some people may mean having a lot of money, being financially independent, and then doing all the things they want to in life. The truth here is that money as an end is never enough. I am not suggesting that looking for success through earning a lot of money first is wrong; if you believe it is the right path, by all means pursue it. I am trying to tell you that there is another way if that path is not working for you. We can also try to start by doing things that make us happy, and it will eventually lead to activities that we love doing, because we will feel more alive and totally involved in our work, and money will eventually come in the process. For example, if you know who you are and what your skills, talents, and strengths are, then adding value through a product or service in the society through what you are best at comes to you naturally.

> "Try not to become a man of success. Rather become a man of value."—Albert Einstein

Reading Books

> "It is what you read when you don't have to that determines what you will be when you can't help it."—Oscar Wilde

Books have been my personal strength. If there is one single habit that has made a tremendous positive difference in my life, I would say it is the habit of reading books. No matter what or how difficult the circumstances in my life have been, I could survive them by reading a few books to understand how I could handle them.

In life we are confused sometimes, and we *have* to be confused, because confusion calls for learning and growth. When we do not understand something or don't know what to do, we are bound to look for answers. These answers could be sought from the opinions of friends, mentors, or older people who have lived wisely and have been there before us. But what people fail to realize is that books have the capacity to help us in every situation, because they contain the experiences of the writer and a great deal of wisdom. All the holy books have been written centuries ago, and yet they can answer any of our modern-day questions. It has been my experience very early in life that the Holy Bible contained all the answers I was seeking. There are other books which are written by writers all through centuries on all the possible subjects we can possibly imagine, and they give great insights on whatever we are seeking, whether it is religion, philosophy, hope, success, politics, money, psychology, animals, or climate change.

> "There is no friend as loyal as a book."—Ernest Hemingway

Books don't talk back, and therefore there is no distraction because we can deduce and make our own, personal interpretations to the thoughts and learning. Our learning will depend on the stage of evolution we stand on in a particular endeavour; we can choose to agree and disagree. We can completely immerse ourselves in to the imagination of the writer—and our own, too—and we can absorb the information with greater focus and concentration. The wise men who have written these books have done it for a reason, and they have left a great deal of knowledge, experience, wisdom, and help for people to take advantage of it.

> "Books are our patient teachers, as they will never give up on us."

Every person has their own capacity of learning. Some people are faster and some are slower, because each person learns things in the right time, and not before or not after. People may not understand you and may give up on you, but books will never do so. They are available for help at any time, and they are patient teachers. Spend enough time reading and rereading them, if necessary.

"To read a book for the first time is to make an acquaintance with a new friend; to read it for the second time is to meet an old one."—Chinese proverb

I have read *Think and Grow Rich, How to Win Friends and Influence People, The Alchemist,* and *The Monk Who Sold the Ferrari* more than five times. Even now, every time I read them, I learn something new, something I could not understand the last time I'd read it, because as I implement what I learn, I am growing as a person daily, and my experience increases my capacity to understand. The changes I feel are amazing and they make me feel more confident. Reading gives me clarity on my thoughts and helps me understand myself.

"Whenever I have found myself lost, a book has found me."

In the last twenty years of my life, I have been through a great deal from my own point of view. Sometimes while looking back, I don't know how I made it through, but I do recall not once but on many occasions that when I did not know what to do, I found a book that answered all my questions and shed light in the darkness. Whenever I feel lost, I walk into a bookstore and go through the books on the shelves. I always walk out of a bookstore with a book. Let me explain how it works for me.

In my life early in school, I loved reading Archie, Tinkle, Readers Digest, The Famous Five, and more. In the late nineties, when the going got tough, I suddenly found myself drawn to books again. During those tough times, I read a few books to maintain my perspective, strength, and inspiration. Books like

You Can Win by Shiv Khera, *Notes to Myself* by Hugh Prather, and *Who Will Cry When You Die* by Robin Sharma had a great impact in my earlier struggles in life, and they always kept me hopeful and motivated. I tried reading a bit from Kahlil Gibran and Arundati Roy; however, I could not comprehend much fifteen years ago—but today, when I read them, I can understand it because I have grown through my struggles and can now relate to these books. In the beginning of 2000, I lost touch with reading books again because that was the time I went through a depression. However, the time I spent reading the books earlier in my life still affected my thought patterns. In the year 2006, when I got married and moved to Dubai, I got involved in a networking business. I didn't know at the time that it was the beginning of my recovery process, but I once again found myself reading books written by successful businessmen like Robert Kiyosaki, Donald Trump, Napoleon Hill, and Richard Branson because I wanted to know and learn from their experiences, attitudes, and decision-making capabilities by entering their world and the way they saw and understood situations. As time went by, I found myself lost and defeated many times, and I was seeking answers again.

I was watching television at 3.00 a.m. one morning, and I saw a brief interview of Joyce Meyer while switching through channels. I learned about her book *Approval Addiction*, but the following day I forgot all about it. While window shopping one day, I walked into a bookstore as usual, and there I saw the only copy of the book in the store, at the bottom of the shelf. I stopped for a moment, trying to understand what was happening, and then I decided maybe it was a sign for me to read this book. I bought and read it, and the book showed me a mirror that horrified me. I immediately understood that my attitude in life towards people needed to change, and I was back in the game.

I will share another example of how I found the book *I Can Make You Rich*. I was shopping with my family in a mall, and after I had finished, I was drawn towards the book section as usual, so I went through the titles and brief descriptions. I came along *I Can Make You Rich* by Paul McKenna. I had not heard of the author, but at the same time I was aware of the limited exposure I had to becoming rich, so I decided to buy the book. I don't know why I bought it; my logic was totally against it, because how could anyone claim to make me rich? It seemed absurd. As a person who anticipates signs, I decided to go against my better judgment. The book went into the bookshelf while I was busy reading other books for about six months.

There came a time one day when I was lost again and didn't know what was happening, so I turned my attention to the bookshelf, and my eyes found this book. It had a self-hypnosis CD to help me program my mind. I did not want to use it because I thought it might make me an evil person, so I decided to only read the book, which did contain a great amount of practical exercises to program my mind. However, because I had not done anything like that before and could not follow it 100 per cent, I decided to be open-minded and listen to the hypnosis CD, to understand how it would help me. Besides, if God had sent this book my way, then there was really no harm accepting it completely and applying it. I began the discipline of listening to the CD, and after a few days I started realizing the small changes in my thinking patterns. I realized the clarity I was getting from this discipline. I was happier, and nothing outward affected my inner peace. Then it dawned on me that self-hypnosis was working on my unconscious behaviour patterns and rewiring my brain. I then recalled reading about positive affirmations in the book *Think and Grow Rich* but did not know how it worked until now. I felt the pieces coming together in my learning, and I felt that as time went by, one book added up to the previous book in a systematic format. I felt like it was a miracle, as if God was teaching me himself, and I could finally put together the pieces of my past, present, and future. Drawn more towards helping people and spirituality then business, I got in touch with my core values, and I decided to share my learning through a book that will help others benefit from my knowledge faster than I did. My learning may not be your learning when you go through these books; you may have your own learning depending on your stage of evolution. If you are brave enough to get lost and seek for answers constantly through books, you will find your way and will know who you are and what you want to do with your life.

"A person who won't read has no advantage over one who can't read."—Mark Twain

Reading is a privilege, and most people have given up on their privileges because they take things for granted, especially when they are free. They look at the cost of the books rather than the invaluable learning, experience, and guidance they provide—and yet they complain of their own self-imposed imprisonment. When we live in an age where we can google all the answers, and access to information is so easily available, we spend time watching a lot of television and making other people richer by exchanging our time and energy patronizing what's unnecessary—instead of sharpening our minds and doing things and learning things that will help us in the long term. Let me share an excellent story which reminds me to keep looking for help.

Luck Favours Those Who Help Themselves

A flood was threatening a small town and everyone was leaving for safety except one man who said, "God will save me. I have faith." As the water level rose a Jeep came to rescue him, the man refused, saying, "God will save me. I have faith." As the water level rose further, he went up to the second storey, and a boat came to help him. Again he refused to go, belying, "God will save me. I have faith." The water kept rising, and the man climbed on to the roof. A helicopter came to rescue him, but he said, "God will save me. I have faith."

Well, finally he drowned. When he reached his maker, he angrily questioned, "I had complete faith in you. Why did you ignore my prayers and let me drown?"

The Lord replied, "Who do you think sent you the Jeep, the boat, and the helicopter?"

This is how we might miss great opportunities. Curiosity leads us to seek answers, and anything that seems like the slightest help must be the answer. If you find yourself seeking for answers, I suggest you pick up a book or spend time in the bookstore. I want you to make a list of the last five books you have read; alternatively, make a list of your problems and challenges, and accordingly make a list of five books to read and go buy them and read them. I will give you a list of books that have helped me at the end of the book; these authors are my mentors.

> "Books were my pass to personal freedom. I learned to read at age three, and soon discovered there was a whole world to conquer that went beyond our farm in Mississippi."—Oprah Winfrey

Create a Mastermind Alliance

There are two ways to learn and pursue your goals. Either you reinvent the wheel, or you find someone who shares your values and interests, and has pursued the same goals as you. Seek someone who has achieved success in your line of work. There is a saying that life is too short to make all the mistakes all over again, and that is true; the former way is painful and long, and the latter way is faster and easier, because you will already hold a point of reference or a benchmark. These masters and gurus can be alive and available in person, or they can be from history and may have written books or recorded audio tapes, leaving their vast knowledge behind for references.

The first path will be very long and painful because you will have no point of reference and expertise available to follow, making it a difficult and long struggle. The second path has a point of reference and expertise available already, with which you can learn and work. It's like when we were children: we learned quickly watching our parents and family, and so we had a point of reference. As humans we naturally have a tendency to learn by watching and simply duplicating what we want to learn.

We Learn consciously through studying, experimenting, and trial and error, like in school, doing things repetitively and consciously until we can master and do the same things competently and unconsciously—for example, learning to say the ABCs and numbers. We can use conscious learning to develop new skills like listening, speaking, and behaving; all we need to do is practice it consciously until it becomes a habit. When a particular behaviour becomes a habit, we will exhibit it effortlessly. Can you imagine the tremendous power we control, to change our life around every twenty-one days and learn a new skill, develop strengths, and be effortlessly competent? If we apply this knowledge and learn something new every month, in a year we will have at least twelve new skills to add to our strengths. Refer to the first chapter to see the list of new skills and behaviours you would like to develop, and take action.

For example, we want to stop using abusive words, and we want to start doing that over the next twenty-one days. In the beginning, since we are used to using swear words, we may fail to consciously remember not to use swear words. We will need to make a conscious effort to remember avoiding swear words all the time in all our discussions. With the passage of time, we will be able to consciously stop using swear words completely.

Conscious learning will also sharpen the short-term memory we need in our daily affairs. Writing goals down starts sharpening our short-term memory, which is important to maintain clarity. For example, we learned in school how to count and read, practicing the skills repetitively, so that we could remember our lessons instinctively with the help of our short-term memory. Conscious learning is a part of our daily life, as we consciously observe ourselves, our behaviour patterns, our perceptions, and our priorities—which will lead us to understand how we talk, walk, and behave. We will be able to improvise to get the desired results. I have therefore personally developed the habit of practicing the sphere of silence daily to accomplish this goal, and I have experienced unbelievable results.

Unconscious learning comes to us naturally, because we are all born with; it means observing and learning things without consciously making an attempt to remember. This is a faster way of learning compared to conscious learning. For example, as children we learn by watching other people around us. Similarly, we can learn a lot of things by spending time with people we admire and want to be like. If they are not physically present, we can watch their videos, exhibiting the skills we want to learn. If we keep watching it over and over again, we will eventually learn those skills unconsciously. For example, have you ever loved and admired a mentor and spent hours with him or watching him? After sometime you find yourself doings things somewhat similar to him. We forget about this gift of learning unconsciously somewhere down the line, when we grow up.

Do you now understand the importance of spending time with the right kind of people, books, and friends? Spend more time with successful people and become successful. If you do not have a role model or a mentor as a benchmark, then you must find one for yourself. To identify one, you will need to visit the chapter "Know Yourself", where you can find out about the kind of shows, movies, friends, and books with which you should be spending more time. For example, if you spend more time with a lie, it eventually becomes the truth. This does not mean you can rule out conscious learning, because the entire learning process is a balance and is a blend of both.

When I was in involved in the network marketing business, I was always asked to watch the basic videos of the business again and again, and I did not understand why that was necessary. Then I realized and understood the human learning process. When I would spend more time hanging around with my mentors and people I admired in the business, I started to realize how I spoke and acted like them unconsciously, sometimes without any effort, only to realize it later. If I had a situation, I would then think about how my mentors would have handled it, and it did give me surprising solutions and a new perspective to the situation. Reading the same books over and over again gave me access to eventually understand and enter the world of the authors, and I received a brand-new perspective. Now, whenever I find myself in a tough spot, I close my eyes and ask myself how would my role models handle this situation? Immediately I get a new and evolved perspective to the challenge.

It is also important to note that unconscious learning can be from the good or bad about a person, and therefore it is important to filter and learn only the positives from your role models. If you have identified your role models, spend a lot of time with them so that you can accelerate your learning process through unconscious learning. If you have not identified your role model, it is okay; keep practicing the "Know Yourself" methods until you are clear about who you are and who you would like to become in the next several months. Read the book *I Can Make You Rich* by Paul McKenna and practice the exercises to get even more clarity.

Life is all about learning daily. A day without learning is like a day without food, and to be healthy you need to have a daily intake of learning and self-correction. If you do not invest in yourself, then do not expect anyone else to as well. A balance in conscious and unconscious learning has to be maintained. Conscious learning is slow, and each person has his or her own pace to learning, so do not compare yourself with others because this will only lead to self-defeat. Unconscious learning is the accelerated learning process; this learning comes to humans naturally and without much effort. Associate yourself with people who share your interests and values, and associate with people who have goals in harmony with your goals. Associate with people who will inspire your quest to achieve your goals. The most important one is to be in harmony with your better half, and involve him or her in your work and help him or her understand your goals and visions. Your loved ones are the closest to you, and remember that the car wheels have to be in alignment for it to be driven smoothly and in the same direction.

Exercising and Meditation

> "Being healthy in mind, body and soul, is the fittest way to be happy."

Health means a lot of different things to different people; it's a relative term, really. Health in general is not only about being fit in the body but also in being fit in your mind and soul. However, being physically fit can enhance health in mind, soul, and finances. A healthy body does influence our state of mind, and that is why health begins with being physically fit first. Spend at least about half an hour a day in the gym. Playing a physical sport, taking a walk, and eating a good diet are good activities with which to begin.

Today we are all the time surrounded by mobiles, computers, televisions, remotes, and other electronics, which have created a great deal of electronic smog in our living and working environments. They emit radiation that is dangerous and harmful to our health, and especially to our children. If we do not feel healthy in our bodies, then there is a higher possibility that we will feel more stressed and have less peace of mind. Physical form of exercise is a fundamental requirement of a healthy body, which will in turn lead to a healthier mind.

In our bodies we also have a natural opium called endorphins; you may want to read up on this before proceeding further. Endorphins are released in our bodies every time we exercise, meditate, laugh, or make love. What endorphins do is create a bonding in the brain cells and make us smarter and sharper; this is another benefit of exercising and meditating that you will experience. Time invested in exercising and meditation is like investing time in you, and results can be great over a period of time, leading you to live a more fulfilled life with clarity, focus, and direction.

Our mind is like a fertile garden, and whatever we sow in it and water daily with patience, we will reap the harvest. Therefore through meditation we have the opportunity to sow peace and calmness by getting in touch with our inner self. When we fail to sow these seeds because we are busy working or have no time for meditation, then weeds will grow in this fertile soil—and then what kind of thoughts do you think we can expect? In today's ever-changing and fast-paced world, it is imperative that we take a minimum of an hour daily to exercise and meditate, so that we can maintain clarity, be centred, and be able to anticipate and seize opportunities quickly. Maintaining clarity in perspective and peace in our minds comes at the cost of self-discipline. We must make use of these beautiful talents God has given us and capitalize on them.

Meditation can be in the form of daydreaming or self-hypnosis; you can also get some great meditational audio CDs. If you can maintain this one hour of discipline daily, do you think your life would change for better? Do you want to have clarity in thoughts? What's stopping you? Whatever answer you get, ask yourself whether it is worth the chance to lose out on a great life for these reasons. If not, then what is the action plan? Write it down and begin immediately. The goal here is to enjoy the process and not worry about the results, because the results will come over a period of time. Have fun, and once your mind and body are liberated, you will feel better, thus changing your entire environment and life by taking charge of yourself.

I started my meditations about a year ago, along with my gym workouts, and I cannot explain the clarity in thoughts, freedom, peace, confidence, and self-belief I have felt since then. I started feeling healthy; I was at peace with myself and those around me, and whatever the situation, I was calm and able to respond quickly. It did take a great deal of self-discipline; the reason self-discipline was not painful was because my desire to become healthy was very strong, and therefore it was easier for me to bear the pain of discipline than to bear the pain of regret. Meditation liberated my mind and gave me greater direction, clarity, and focus on tasks. Since then, whenever I find myself challenged, I quietly move back to a quiet place to meditate. Meditation also helped me get rid of the weeds in my mind and replace them with thoughts that are helpful for me on an unconscious level; it was like rewiring my mind and reprogramming my central processing unit with new and helpful programs. This is how powerful meditations have been for me. Isn't it amazing to feel that you have the power to control your life and the direction it will take?

"The only battle you need to win is within, the only person you need to conquer is yourself and the only person you need to be is you so that you can live your life to its full potential." Here is a small story to explain why.

Start with Yourself

When I was young and free and my imagination had no limits, I dreamed of changing the world. As I grew older and wiser, I discovered the world would not change, so I shortened my sights somewhat and decided to change only my country.

But it, too, seemed immovable.

As I grew into my twilight years, in one last desperate attempt, I settled for changing only my family, those closest to me, but alas, they would have none of it.

And now as I lie on my deathbed, I suddenly realize: If I had only changed myself first, then by example I would have changed my family.

From their inspiration and encouragement, I would then have been able to better my country, and who knows, I may have even changed the world.

Start working on yourself within first, and live inside out. For references, I have mentioned the books at the end of the book.

GOD'S PLAN

"There are only two ways to live your life.
One is as though nothing is a miracle.
The other is as though everything is a miracle."
—Albert Einstein

God's plan begins the day we are born in a particular family, with our set of circumstances that we have not chosen. We grow up in this environment with our experiences, perceptions, and aspirations. We grow up to be a person with a set of skills, talents, strengths, and weaknesses; we are unique because of this and therefore have been prepared by God for a particular task for the future. Every experience or setback is a preparation for what's to come. Life is like a treasure hunt: one clue leads to the other, and everything is connected. Our eyes are the windows through which we see and perceive the world, so what we see in the world will depend on our experiences, whether it is with love, friendship, family, community, or politics. Along this journey, we also have our aspirations and dreams. God's plan is always about following God's will as opposed to our free will; there is a reason why we are where we are today. Our friends, neighbours, colleagues, enemies, challenges, and learning are all a part of the design in the master plan for us to learn and play our role.

Following God's will requires us to make God the point of reference in everything that we do, so that we may never stray away from him. Our heart contains the seed for God's plan; all we have to do is follow our hearts and not our mind, which is full of logic. Our logic is based on our limited experiences and has a limited perspective and belief. If we live our lives by logic, we will never be able to accomplish much in life. When we want something from our heart, our logic cannot comprehend; like love or passion, they cannot be understood, they can only be felt, and they bring about more enthusiasm and excitement. An amazing power takes over us, and time stands still. If we can only let these tiny sparks in our hearts turn into fire, then we will then live a more fulfilled and accomplished life. God has a plan for all living creatures and mankind. We are interdependent on each other: nature provides us with its bounty, while each animal has a different purpose.

Similarly, we humans have our own purpose in each other's lives. Our actions, words, and decisions do impact the people around us; we are all playing our roles in each other's lives, and we are a part of the master plan and are interwoven in the fabric of society. For example, if I have a fight with someone, that person might go and fight with other people, and in turn those people will fight with others, creating a ripple effect. If I spent money on something, that money will flow from one hand to another, constantly providing for someone. Similarly, if we spread happiness and joy, it will spread. Whatever we give out goes to many out there, directly and indirectly.

We are unique, and the day we know our core values, we will wake up to new existence and will fall in line with our purpose in life. I was a waiter for three years, had a heart break, became a disc jockey, met my wife, and moved to the corporate world. I needed to take a break from all the legal issues, sailed on a passenger cruise ship, lost that job, and came back to take care of legal matters. I lost my house and was pushed to buy my new two-bedroom apartment. Yolanda got a job in Dubai, and we moved to Dubai. I started working a network marketing business as our first child, Daniel, was due, and I needed an additional income. I worked the business for four years, and in the process I recovered from my depression through the help I received from my mentors and the books I read. I discovered what my core values are, who I really am, and what my purpose in life is. I put the pieces of the jigsaw puzzle of my life together, which had unfolded over the last twenty years. God is looking after us even through our adversities, and therefore we must not doubt his wisdom. Let me explain this with this beautiful short story about why we should trust God and have faith in him—and not our own intelligence.

Two Travelling Angels

Two travelling angels stopped to spend the night in the home of a wealthy family. The family was rude and refused to let the angels stay in the mansion's guest room. Instead the angels were given a small space in the cold basement.

As they made their bed on the hard floor, the older angel saw a hole in the wall and repaired it. When the younger angel asked why, the older angel replied, "Things aren't always what they seem."

The next night the pair came to rest at the house of a very poor but very hospitable farmer and his wife.

After sharing what little food they had, the couple let the angels sleep in their bed, where they could have a good night's rest.

When the sun came up the next morning, the angels found the farmer and his wife in tears. Their only cow, whose milk had been their sole income, lay dead in the field.

The younger angel was infuriated and asked the older angel, "How could you have let this happen? The first man had everything, yet you helped him," she accused. "The second family had little but was willing to share everything, and you let the cow die."

"Things aren't always what they seem," the older angel replied. "When we stayed in the basement of the mansion, I noticed there was gold stored in that hole in the wall. Since the owner was so obsessed with greed and unwilling to share his good fortune, I sealed the wall so he wouldn't find it. Then last night, as we slept in the farmer's bed, the angel of death came for his wife. I gave him the cow instead. Things aren't always what they seem."

Sometimes that is exactly what happens when things don't turn out the way they should. If you have faith, you just need to trust that every outcome is always to your advantage. You just might not know it until sometime later.

I think this short story will put a lot of things in perspective. I have finally made sense of my past and am using it to design my present and my future. Do you want to know what your purpose in life is?

Stop making sense and follow God's plan!

AUTHOR BIO
LAWRENCE KINNY

I started with humble beginnings with a Job as a waiter to support my studies. Gradually with the love and passion for music and a heart break, ventured into show business and became a successful Disc Jokey, popularly known as DJ Larry. Interviewed on Music Asia & Channel V in the year 2000, also had write-ups in major tabloids like Bombay times & Mid-day. After seven years of Stardom and glamour I made an important decision to move to the corporate world after meeting my soul mate and my wife now Yolanda in 2001. I started with a BPO, as a customer service representative, the culture of the corporate world was too scary and so I became a sailor on an international cruise liner as a part of the production team. I sailed about for one and half year saw the world got paid for it and enjoyed every bit of it. I moved back to land with another backend customer service job in 2004 worked there for about a year and a half, bought my own two bedroom apartment, got Married and moved to Dubai and worked with a bank. I then realized that I was handling other peoples money, and I thought to myself why not me? got involved in a business. In the business I was introduced to the most amazing person I have met, ME. I realized I had to find a way to fulfill my values, goals & work in alignment and then answered the call of being an Author. I currently live in Dubai; I have two beautiful children Daniel and Sarah and grateful to God for shaping me up with all the opportunities he gave me.

List of books I recommend reading.
1) The Alchemist 'Paulo Coelho'
2) The Secret 'Rhonda Byrne'
3) Think and grow rich 'Napolean Hill'
4) Rich dad poor dad 'Robert Kiyosaki'
5) Cash flow quadrant 'Robert kiyosaki'
6) Why we want you to be rich 'Robert Kiyosaki and Donald Trump'
7) I can make you rich 'Paul Mckenna'
8) Four hour work week 'Timothy Ferris'
9) Awaken the giant within 'Anthony Robins'
10) The monk who sold the Ferrari 'Robin Sharma'
11) The leader without a title 'Robin Sharma'
12) Power of now 'Eckhart tolle'
13) How to win friends and influence people 'Dale carnegie'